GILDED AGE
MURDER & MAYHEM
in the
BERKSHIRES

ANDREW K. AMELINCKX

THE
History
PRESS

Published by The History Press
Charleston, SC 29403
www.historypress.net

Copyright © 2015 by Andrew K. Amelinckx
All rights reserved

First published 2015

ISBN 978.1.54021.248.1

Library of Congress Control Number: 2015947037

CONTENTS

CONTENTS

ACKNOWLEDGEMENTS

This book would not have been possible without the dedication, support and hard work of my wife, Kara Thurmond, who acted as ringmaster to my circus of words. I'd like to thank our families, who have always been behind us and our flights of fancy. Thanks to Tabitha Dulla and the rest of the editors from The History Press for giving me this opportunity. A special thanks goes to the *Berkshire Eagle* for use of its images and the Berkshire Athenaeum with its wondrous collection of local lore. And I must not forget to thank the ladies (and gentleman) of the Pittsfield District Court Clerk's Office who made my time as a crime reporter in the Berkshires that much better.

INTRODUCTION

The Berkshires of Massachusetts in the Gilded Age, the period that runs roughly from 1870 to the early 1900s, was an anomaly. It was a wild and wooly backwoods on the state's western border as well as a playground for New York City's wealthy elite, with a cosmopolitan flair, rich cultural history and long record of scientific innovation in industry.

Crime in the Berkshires during this time was also anomalous. Unlike today, it was the small, rural areas that saw the most lawlessness, while the larger population centers—Pittsfield, North Adams and Great Barrington—were relatively quiet.

In 1893, Waldo L. Cook, who would later become the editor of the *Springfield Republican* newspaper, wrote an article for the American Statistical Association on murders in Massachusetts covering the years 1871 to 1892. Cook found that of the ten first- and second-degree murder convictions between 1871 and 1892 in western Massachusetts—the twenty towns that are located in the region contain only a quarter of the population that the six cities Pittsfield, North Adams, Springfield, Northampton, Chicopee and Holyoke do—had twice as many murders as the cities combined. Specifically, in Berkshire County during that period, there were five murders. They all took place in the county's small towns, including Otis, Sheffield and Washington, whose populations were in decline. The county's largest city, Pittsfield, saw no murders during that same period.

What's interesting is that while the population of the county grew by twenty thousand people from 1870 to 1890, going from around sixty-five to

A scenic view of the Berkshires from the early twentieth century. *Courtesy of the Library of Congress.*

eighty-five thousand, the homicide rate decreased. But (and there is always a but) when compared to the rest of the state during that period, the western counties, of which Berkshire is one, saw a bigger increase in per capita homicides than in other parts of the commonwealth. "One finds certain rural counties having a decidedly stronger tendency toward the homicidal crimes than the metropolitan district," he remarked.

The term "the Gilded Age" was coined by Samuel Clemens, better known as Mark Twain, and Charles Dudley Warner in their satirical 1873 novel *The Gilded Age: A Tale of Today,* which poked fun at the era's materialism and political corruption. The term itself is evocative of the period's love of ostentatious decoration as well as the tendency to cover society's ills with an air of respectability, like a cheap piece of furniture covered by a thin veneer of gilding.

The criminal justice system was much different one hundred–plus years ago, as I learned while researching the stories. For instance, anyone today who has seen a courtroom drama is familiar with opening statements in which the opposing lawyers each take turns giving their version of the facts to the jury. In Massachusetts in the nineteenth century, the prosecution would give an opening statement and then present its evidence to the all-male jury (women wouldn't be allowed to sit on a jury in Massachusetts until 1950). When the district attorney's case was finished, the defense would then give their opening statement and evidence. Other oddities included some trials where there were several judges hearing the case at once. As in today's grand jury proceedings, but unlike trials, jurors were allowed to ask questions of the witnesses. Additionally, the state's attorney general personally handled capital murder cases, something unheard of in Massachusetts today.

Another interesting facet of the era was the amount of access the press had to crime scenes, the police and criminals awaiting trial. Reporters were often at the crime scene or, more accurately, in the crime scene with investigators as they looked for clues. The police often shared whatever information they'd gathered about a case with the press, and reporters prowled around the jails looking for an interview with any prisoner who caught their interest, and in most cases, without consulting their counsels, the defendants would oblige. This practice dovetails with the stark difference between a defendant's rights back in the Gilded Age and today. Back in the nineteenth and early twentieth centuries, the country's justice system was quick, often brutal, and the scales were weighed in favor of the prosecution. On the other hand, plea bargaining became a norm during this period. (In two of the stories in this book, defendants pleaded guilty to second-degree murder to avoid the death penalty.) But on the whole, defendants didn't have the same rights as they enjoy today.

During the years covered in this book, another change took place. Before 1900, executions were handled in Massachusetts by the county jails, with hanging being the preferred method. By the turn of the century, the state solidified control of the process, and deaths by the newfangled electric chair were conducted in Boston.

This book, which contains fourteen stories, is broken up into five parts: "Love Gone Bad and Just Plain Greed," "Lessons in Temperance," "Accidents and Incidents," "The Ones That Got Away" and "Axes and Barkers" (barker being the slang expression for a gun in the nineteenth century). I wanted the book to have an older feel, and these various categories, for me, have a dime novel (called a penny dreadful in England) ring to them. "Dime novel" and "penny dreadful" were terms used in the nineteenth century to describe pulp stories that were snapped up by mostly working-class boys and young men and focused on somewhat lurid tales of criminals and detectives.

I spaced the stories out as far as the various years encompassed by the Gilded Age, so the reader will notice that the stories are not presented chronologically but rather are grouped by general theme. The final story in this book, "The Trolley Car Killings," takes place in 1911, at the very end of the period. There seems to be some debate on the years encompassed by the period, but I felt it was a story that marked the end of the era and the true beginning of the twentieth century, which would see violence on a scale those in the nineteenth century couldn't have even imagined.

Part 1

LOVE GONE BAD
AND JUST PLAIN GREED

The Berkshire County Courthouse, circa 1900. It's still in use today. *Courtesy of the Library of Congress.*

THE GENTLEMAN BURGLAR

STOCKBRIDGE

Charles Southmayd was awakened from a sound sleep by shouts of "the house is on fire!" Running to his bedroom door, he threw it open. There before him stood a man wearing a black mask around the lower part of his face and towels wrapped around his shoes to muffle his footfalls. He was the one who had sounded the false alarm.

The seventy-year-old Southmayd put up a pretty good fight, but the burglar, younger and stronger, threw the old lawyer to the ground, ransacked the bedroom and made off with $200 cash (about $4,800 in today's terms) and quickly made his escape.

He may have not behaved like a gentleman in this instance, but in other crimes in the fall of 1892 and summer of 1893, the burglar's soothing voice and civility showed when he confronted several female homeowners. They reported that his voice and manners put them at ease as the six-foot-tall masked man pointed his gun at them and went through their rooms looking for loot. One of his female victims, who awoke to find a man in a derby hat with a kerchief covering the lower part of his face, was so charmed by his manners she was quoted in the *New York Times* as saying she would "dislike to know he was taken up." The woman was a servant in one of the grand "cottages" of the wealthy New Yorkers who summered in Stockbridge.

Another of the robber's female victims described the man's hands as being "small, delicately shaped and unused to hard work." A third victim, Kate

The Southmayd farm in Stockbridge where Charles Southmayd struggled with the gentleman burglar. *Photograph by author.*

Stetson, mentioned his fashionable attire. His three-button cutaway coat "fit him to a nicety," the woman later remarked. She said his eyes were "dark, and mild and soft of expression." His ears—yes, she noticed his ears—were "small and shapely."

Stetson was a guest of Lillian Swan, who was from a prominent New York family, that night in June 1893 when the gentleman burglar came a-calling at the Parke Cottage, located on Main Street in Stockbridge. Swan had taken out a large sum of cash from the bank that day to be used for a shopping spree in New York City. When Stetson arrived at about 9:00 p.m., her escort handed her a pistol, urging her to take it for protection.

"You may have need of it before morning," he said, handing the weapon to her. The two friends were the only occupants of the residence that night. Stetson stepped into the cottage and handed the pistol to Swan. "This is safer with you," she told the other woman.

"Don't mind it if you hear any noise. I'm going to pack my trunk and propose to read before retiring," Lillian told her guest as Kate headed to bed. The women's rooms were just across the main hall from each other. A few hours later, Stetson woke to a grating noise that sounded like drawers were being roughly pulled open and closed. She rubbed the sleep from her eyes and continued listening, sweat beginning to cover her body. The noise continued and seemed to be coming from the hall. "Lillian!" she called out.

The noise continued. "Lillian, is that you?" she called out again. She yelled her friend's name a third time. It wasn't her friend who now stood in her doorway, a derby hat perched on his head and a mask covering the lower part of his face. The lamp he held in his hand threw eerie shadows around the room. In the stranger's other hand was a pistol, which was aimed in her direction. He stood there for what seemed like ages. Stetson could neither speak nor move for the terror she felt. She later recalled that the man seemed to take pleasure in the fear he inspired. Finally, he spoke.

"Be quiet! I won't hurt you," he told her in a slow, deliberate cadence. "If you make a noise, I will shoot you." His low voice—soothing, almost musical, mesmerizing—snapped Kate out of her paralysis, and the tension vanished. There was a 180-degree change in the room like "a passing summer breeze" as the stifling silent presence now become a speaking human.

Stetson's third shout of Swan's name had roused the woman from sleep. Just then, Lillian called out from her room. "Kate, what is it?"

Stetson said nothing as she stared at the intruder and the barrel of his pistol, which was still aimed at her.

"Kate, Kate! What is it? What is it?"

"It is the man," Stetson finally replied to her friend.

"I want your money," he told her as he began digging around the dresser, adding there was no point in resisting because he had six men downstairs.

"I have none," she replied coolly. "I only came to spend the night with my friend because she is afraid of you. No one in Stockbridge keeps money in their homes nowadays because they are afraid of you."

The stranger didn't reply but arched his eyebrows in response—a movement he made often, according to his victims. He collected a few pennies from her dresser and left the room without another word. He then slipped into Swan's room and was greeted by Lillian, who was sitting up in bed with the pistol Kate had given her earlier that night clenched in her hand.

"I have a pistol," she told the man.

"So have I," he retorted, stepping closer.

"But I'll shoot," she responded.

He continued to move toward her, telling her he didn't believe she would shoot.

"You'd better give me that pistol," he told her. "You might hurt yourself with it."

She answered she couldn't give it to him because the gun was borrowed. He promised to leave the weapon downstairs. When she asked if he could leave it in the hall, he refused.

He was so close now, she could have reached out and touched him. She could have slipped the mask from his face. Instead, she handed him the weapon.

As the burglar rifled through her possessions, Lillian asked him why he didn't find another line of work. He didn't answer and only gave her an icy stare.

After some more repartee between the two, the thief left with an emerald ring, the woman's watch and some cash and then returned to Kate's room. Stetson had hidden her watch under her pillow but had transferred it to her person after the stranger with the cool, dark eyes had left to visit her friend's room.

Reentering Kate's room, he asked her where she had hidden her watch. She lied and said she had left it at home in the fear that he might come. As he turned to leave, Stetson, hoping to glean more identifying characteristics from the burglar, called out to him.

"Oh, are you going?" she asked him. "What are you going to do now?"

He turned, walked back toward her bed and looked at her intently before quickly turning and leaving the room.

Both women jumped out of bed and followed the burglar down the stairs and onto the first floor. They watched him walk out of the back door, the same way he had gained entrance into the house. The burglar hopped onto a buggy driven by several fast horses and made his escape. But the gentleman burglar had more business in town that night. The women waited an hour, fearing his return, and then sounded the alarm. They opened the window and screamed for help. None came that night.

Main Street in Stockbridge, Massachusetts, today. *Photograph by author.*

MRS. FIELD'S WATCH

Most of the New York society women on vacation in Stockbridge whom the burglar targeted demurred to his requests—this was the Victorian era after all—but Laura Field, the daughter-in-law of the eminent law reformer David Dudley Field, put up one hell of a struggle to try to keep a watch worth $1,500 (close to $40,000 in today's terms).

It was the bandit's second housebreak on the night of June 16, 1893, the first was the break-in and robbery at the Parke Cottage. He slipped unseen into the Fields' Laurel Cottage, also on Main Street, through a window and made his way around the home and into Laura's bedroom. She awoke with a start; there was a hand over her mouth and hot breath on her face. The robber was on his knees, groping around the bed looking for any hidden loot. When his hand found the watch she had hidden under her pillow, any fear Laura had was replaced by anger.

"You shan't have my watch," she screeched, throwing her arms around his neck.

"Be quiet," he told her, putting the barrel of his gun against her forehead, "or I shall shoot you."

He straightened up to his full height, but Laura held on, clinging to him, her feet no longer touching the ground.

He argued with her, pleaded and told her she would be hurt, but she continued to fight him. The fracas woke a valet who ran into the hall where the robber was trying to make his escape, Laura still hanging from his neck.

"Shoot," she shouted. "Don't mind me! Shoot!"

The valet stood paralyzed, pistol in hand, before turning around and heading back into his room, mumbling something about getting his robe. The robber finally heaved Laura off, throwing her into a wall, and made his escape out the back door. The valet, now wearing his robe, rushed down the stairs and wildly fired a bullet through the closed front door.

Stockbridge was soon in a state of high anxiety. The citizenry barred their doors and locked their windows, and the menfolk stayed up half the night, guns in their hands, waiting for the gentleman burglar to try to break into their homes. The wealthiest in town hired private security. A *New York Times* reporter who went there that September said that, after dark, the town became an "armed band of resistance." Even "strong-nerved" women had abandoned their nighttime prayer meetings unless accompanied by a male escort, and men did not go out past 8:00 p.m. unless armed.

Above: Downtown Stockbridge, Massachusetts, with the well-known Red Lion Inn on the right. *Photograph by author.*

Left: David Dudley Field, the eminent law reformer, who owned one of the homes that was ransacked by the gentleman burglar. Field's daughter-in-law, Laura, attempted to fight off the intruder. *Courtesy of the Library of Congress.*

By this time, a $1,200 reward (more than $30,000 in today's terms) had been placed on the rogue's head, but still he eluded capture.

In November, the gentleman burglar and three cohorts were involved in a break-in of the rectory of the Episcopal church in Lenox, where four gold watches were stolen, as well as an attempted robbery of a store. This was the last of the gentleman burglar's escapades in the Berkshires. The men stole a carriage and boarded a train bound for New York City at Chatham, a town just across the border from Berkshire County.

New York

This smooth-talking, gun-toting thief next turned up in Long Island City, Queens, in November 1893. The burglars were soon terrorizing the citizens of Queens and Long Island after moving south from their spree in Stockbridge, mostly preying on the same caliber of very wealthy victims as those in Massachusetts. And like their New England brethren, the folks in New York had begun carrying guns, patrolling the streets and sleeping with their weapons by their sides—with similar results. The gentleman burglar and his cronies were too slick to be caught by amateurs.

It wasn't until nearly two months after the last of the Berkshires break-ins that the man police believed was responsible for the crimes was captured. Michael Sherlock and two members of his gang were cornered by police at gunpoint at the Thirty-fourth Street ferry house in Queens, New York, as they tried to make their escape to Manhattan on New Year's Eve. They had just robbed a courier from a nearby packinghouse.

It was an earlier burglary in Maspeth, Long Island, that helped bring down the master criminal and his partners. A few days before Christmas, Sherlock and one of his cohorts, Michael Mahoney, broke into the house of Christopher Meyer and his two unwed sisters while the women were alone in the house following an outing in Brooklyn. One of the sisters, Elizabeth Meyer, woke up to a man's hand under her pillow. She screamed, waking her sister, Annie, who begged the men not to kill them. The tall stranger told the women in a soothing tone that they would not be hurt and that he and his friend were only there for their valuables. The two men made off with cash and jewelry amounting to more than $100,000 in today's terms.

The burglary was big news since the women were the sisters of Cord Meyer, a rich property developer and a chairman of the New York State

Democratic Committee who had recently run for New York secretary of state. He was instrumental in developing the Long Island towns of Elmhurst and Forest Hills. His grandson, also named Cord Meyer, was a CIA agent and writer allegedly involved in a plot to assassinate President John F. Kennedy.

Preying on the super wealthy and well connected probably helped in the gentleman burglar's downfall, as the police seemed to be working overtime to nab him. They developed information, based in part on the victims' descriptions of the culprits, and began surveilling Sherlock's movements. A reporter for the *Evening World*, a New York newspaper, called the police's task keeping tabs on Sherlock "a long and trying job" since the criminal was "an ingenious rascal of the type who sleeps with one eye open and is always alert to avoid contact with the police." Nevertheless, the rascal apparently let his greed overtake his common sense and set up another job just days after the Meyer break-in.

Police tailed Sherlock for days and took note of the people the thirty-four-year-old Astoria, Queens resident and streetcar driver spent time with. The detectives learned from an informant that Sherlock and his cohorts were planning to knock over the Astoria Packing Company. Police staked out the building, but to no avail since Sherlock and his men had decided it was too risky. On the night they had decided to do the job, there were too many people in the area because of a wake and a ball near the building. Instead, they waited a few days and then robbed one of the employees after he left the business at night carrying a change box with about $76 ($2,000 today) in cash inside. Sherlock waited for the man to exit the building and then clubbed him and made off with the strongbox.

The man quickly recovered and sounded the alarm. Two other employees who were sleeping at the warehouse came running out in their slippers carrying large knives and a pistol. Seven shots rang out, but all missed the fleeing robbers. One of the employees who chased after the robbers turned a corner and ran into Sherlock. The burglar struck the man with a blackjack, knocking him out cold.

A few hours later Sherlock, Mahoney and Edward Fitzgerald—a former police constable who had become a criminal—were taken into custody when two detectives recognized Sherlock and walked up to the men at the ferry terminal. They thrust their guns in the men's faces and ordered them to put their hands up. It wasn't quite the end of the line for Sherlock though. He and his friends were released for a lack of evidence, and the two detectives were busted down the ranks, apparently due to the political pull of Sherlock and his cohorts.

Not long after Sherlock's arrest, several other burglars were picked up in Bridgeport, Connecticut, and there was some talk that perhaps the gang's leader—Thomas "Big Tom" Kinsella Jr., a Stockbridge native who served time for accidentally shooting and killing his mother-in-law in 1887—was the "real" gentleman burglar. The newspapers debated the subject; the consensus was that Sherlock most deserved the infamous appellation. It was believed that Kinsella was the leader of the gang, of which Sherlock was a member, terrorizing Stockbridge. When Kinsella and his men were arrested in Connecticut, Fitzgerald, the ex-police constable, was shot and later died from his wounds. Police believed Sherlock, a month after escaping justice in Long Island City, had been involved in the Bridgeport break-ins but had eluded capture when the other men were taken into custody.

The Tightening Net

In April, it really was the end of the line for the gentleman burglar. New York City police were keeping a close watch on Sherlock and believed there was enough evidence to tie him to the Berkshire home invasions as well as the break-in of the Meyer residence on Long Island. They contacted authorities in Massachusetts, who sent a warrant, and then nabbed Sherlock and yet another cohort, Christopher Madden, a ruffian described as "hideous in appearance" due to his lower lip having been torn off in an earlier bar brawl with a reporter. Madden was held while police tried to hunt up enough evidence to charge him. Sherlock was shipped back to Massachusetts.

Back in the Berkshires, police—and the famed Pinkerton's National Detective Agency—recovered much of the loot taken in the Stockbridge burglaries, including Laura Field's watch, which was described as small and of Swiss make with a blue enamel case encrusted with diamonds. It was the handiwork of the Pinkerton detective George S. Dougherty that led to the recovery of the items. It was never revealed how Dougherty, the man credited with making fingerprinting suspects a standard police procedure, was able to recover the goods. The Pinkerton Agency was the first, biggest and best detective and private security firm in the nation and was so well regarded that the U.S. government used it against the Confederacy during the Civil War. The agency's logo, which featured a human eye and the tag line "We Never Sleep," was where the term "private eye" originated.

Although Sherlock and Kinsella escaped justice in the New York break-ins thanks to the untimely death of Kinsella's estranged wife, who planned to testify against them, both men wound up in prison. Kinsella served fifteen years in Connecticut for the series of Bridgeport burglaries, and Sherlock went down for the Lenox and Stockbridge crimes. At trial, Sherlock said he had once been a special police officer whose job was to "preserve order at picnics" and swore he had never been in Berkshire County until being hauled there for trial. He admitted he knew the other men accused of the crimes. The jury apparently didn't fall for the story. He was sentenced to fifteen years in prison with one day in solitary—a bonus for attempting to saw through the bars of his jail cell in Pittsfield while he awaited trial.

2

THE CUCKOLD KILLER

Blood on the Road

"Oh God, George, you will forgive me, won't you?" were Gertrude Huber's last words, spoken to her husband, who had just shot her in the back. She lay sprawled out on a road in Monterey, Massachusetts. George, his anger at his wife's infidelity dissipated, held her in his arms as she bled to death on the morning of September 14, 1902. "I forgive you," he told the twenty-two-year-old woman before she died.

Huber had tracked his wife from their home in New York City to this small town about eight miles east of Great Barrington after she had run off with a young and handsome professional magician and vaudeville singer named Andrew Fearing. The fugitive couple had been on the run for five weeks and ended up in Massachusetts, where they had been staying at a summer boardinghouse under the names Mr. and Mrs. Fearing.

Huber had arrived two days earlier and was boarding at the home of Deputy Sheriff William Bidwell. Like his wife, Huber was less than honest about his identity. He told the deputy he was named William Murphy. Huber apparently confided, at least in part, what was going on to the lawman, who urged him not to take matters into his own hands but rather to let the authorities handle it. Since Fearing and Gertrude were committing the crime of adultery, they could be arrested. Huber may not have trusted Bidwell to act since the New Yorker had already been rebuffed by a local judge who had refused to issue a warrant of arrest against the couple.

The day before the killing, Huber had finally spotted Gertrude and had been spying on the couple's goings on at the hotel where they were staying with some friends, Mr. and Mrs. Costello, who were also in the entertainment business. Just a few days before the shooting, Fearing and Costello had performed magic tricks for the Christian Endeavor Society.

The morning of the murder, Huber waited outside the boardinghouse, hidden in the bushes, and when Gertrude, Fearing and the Costellos went for a walk in the hopes of enjoying the beautiful fall weather, Huber sprang upon them from behind.

"Gert, what does this mean?" Huber angrily asked his startled wife, who turned around at the sound of her husband's voice. Fearing also turned around, and when he saw Huber, he pointed at Gertrude, saying. "There she is. There she is."

Something snapped inside Huber when he heard Fearing's voice. He pulled a revolver from his hip pocket and fired at Fearing, who ran for the bushes. The bullet struck him, but he kept running farther into the underbrush. Huber turned to his unfaithful wife, who had begun running in the opposite direction of Fearing, and called to her to stop. As the terrified woman continued to run, all the anger, frustration and jealousy welled up at once in Huber. He raised the weapon and fired a single shot. The bullet struck Gertrude just below the left shoulder blade, ripping through her. She fell face forward but was caught by her husband, who had rushed toward her after firing the shot. The owner of the boardinghouse witnessed the shooting and came over to where Huber, now hysterical, sat with his dead wife and closed Gertrude's eyes. Huber accosted a carriage driver, insisting he take the body to the deputy's house, but the growing crowd of onlookers insisted the body stay where it lay. Bidwell was called for and soon arrived.

"Why didn't you wait? I could have arranged things in a couple of days," the deputy told Huber before taking him into custody.

No one was aware that Fearing had been shot until he was taken into custody. The bullet had gone through his right arm just above the elbow. A doctor was called to attend the young man. Literally adding insult to injury, Fearing was charged for his adulterous behavior with Gertrude. Both men were arraigned later that week in the district court in Great Barrington before Judge Walter Sanford (the same judge to whom Huber had originally requested help in obtaining arrest warrants for the fugitive couple). The defendants pleaded not guilty to the charges and were held at the Berkshire County Jail and House of Correction in Pittsfield pending grand jury proceedings.

Prelude to a Murder

Gertrude Rentel Huber was born in Prussia and immigrated with her parents to the United States in 1885 when she was five, arriving in New York on the passenger ship *Moravia*. The family settled in Brooklyn, where her father, Rudolph Rentel, made a decent living operating a candy store.

According to Gertrude's father, Huber had begun courting his only child, whom they called Trude, when she was just sixteen years old after the two met at a German church picnic. Huber—whose first name was actually Gottlieb, but who went by George, the Anglicized version of his name—was also of German descent. While Rudolph tried to keep Huber, who was nearly twice his daughter's age, away from Gertrude, there was no controlling the lovesick girl. Rather than risk losing her altogether, Trude's parents allowed her to leave with Huber when she turned eighteen. George and Gertrude took off for Buffalo and then ended up in Chicago.

"She was only a child and believed all the promises of happiness he made her," Rentel would later recall. "He had a fine manner and was a good talker."

After leaving New York, Trude lied to her parents, telling them she and Huber had tied the knot—even giving them the name of a fictitious church in Jersey City, New Jersey—but her father found out the truth after doing a little digging. When the couple returned to New York in October 1898, after nearly a year away, Rentel forced them to get married for real in a small church ceremony held on Washington Avenue in Brooklyn. According to Huber, he had tried to get Gertrude to marry him on several occasions while they were living in Chicago, but she had refused.

Back in New York, the couple made their home in several spots, bouncing between Manhattan and Brooklyn. Gertrude's father gave Huber $200 (more than $5,000 today) that he invested in a shooting gallery on Coney Island's famed boardwalk, but a fire (Coney Island was infamous for fires) burned the arcade to the ground along with any further hopes for the business venture. Huber next turned to making awnings for a living and eventually had a shop below the apartment where he and Gertrude lived on West 124th Street in Manhattan.

According to Huber, his marriage to Gertrude was rocky, but he loved her too much to break it off. They fought on a regular basis about her infidelities. During one of their rows, Gertrude picked up her husband's revolver and fired at him several times, but Huber, fearing that this might happen, had put blanks in the gun. Afterward, she became hysterical and began banging her head into the wall until Huber physically restrained her.

FOR MORE THAN A YEAR before the murder, Fearing had been seeing Gertrude on the sly. He often visited Gertrude at her home for their rendezvous, and a free meal or two, when her husband was out working and would leave before Huber arrived home. Trude told the landlady Fearing was her brother to allay any suspicions. Huber eventually found out about what was going on and confronted his philandering wife. She broke down, admitted her wrongdoing and begged forgiveness. Huber gave in and, for a while, peace again descended on the household. After the first incident, Huber believed the two lovers had stopped seeing each other, but one evening when returning from a job, he spied the pair entering an apartment building on Seventh Avenue in Manhattan. The building was nicknamed "Bachelor's Headquarters," and Fearing, whom Huber referred to as "that bum concert singer," rented a room there. Huber later found out that Trude paid for the place. Huber again forgave his wife, and things seemed to return to normal until the day he returned home to find his wife gone without explanation.

When Huber went to her parents' home in Brooklyn to get answers, the couple lied to him, saying they had no idea where their daughter had gone. The truth was that Gertrude had come to her father a few days before she left town with paperwork showing that Huber was still legally married to another woman.

"I fear he is going to kill me for I've found out," she told her father.

Trude lied to her parents, telling them she was going to Massachusetts to be a lady's companion for a rich widow when she was actually running off with her lover. Huber later claimed he had been married when he was very young but had been granted a divorce. He was amazingly short on details as to his first marriage and the supposed divorce. He claimed not to even remember his first wife's name. He never did produce any papers proving he wasn't still married to the woman, whose name was Mary Levine.

When Gertrude's father went to collect some furniture from Huber's Harlem apartment, the younger man again tried to shake him down for information on Trude's whereabouts.

"I'll kill her even if I'm put away for twenty years," Huber warned the older man.

Rentel took the threat seriously because of Huber's past. His son-in-law had shot a man to death on Myrtle Street in Brooklyn several years prior. Huber had been convicted of manslaughter and, after serving a short stint in prison, had been pardoned by Governor David B. Hill.

The newspapers in Massachusetts, which tended to side with Huber, alluded to his shady past but were vague on details. The New York papers, which generally took Gertrude's side in the matter (after all, she had been murdered), made more of Huber's criminal history.

A few weeks after Huber's confrontation with Gertrude's father, Huber was shown a letter from Fearing written to a mutual friend of both men in which Fearing claimed Gertrude had not come to Massachusetts with him. Fearing also bragged in the letter that if Huber showed up in Monterey, he'd get what he deserved. Huber now had a solid lead after weeks of spinning his wheels in New York. Even if it turned out his wife wasn't in Monterey, he could at least settle the score

New York governor David B. Hill. *Courtesy of Wikimedia Commons.*

with Fearing. Huber sent a letter to Gertrude's parents letting them know he was going to Massachusetts to retrieve his wife. Fearing may have also sent the letter to gloat about his news.

Rentel wrote to his daughter, warning her that Huber was on her trail, but the letter arrived a day too late to help Gertrude. The family's next piece of news about the girl was in the form of a telegram from the coroner informing the family that she was dead.

The Aftermath

Huber, who was being held without bail, sat in jail awaiting the outcome of negotiations between his defense team and the district attorney. Huber frequently spoke to reporters, telling them how miserable he was about killing his wife. He also admitted that he regretted only having winged Fearing.

"I couldn't help it. Perhaps I'm crazy—I don't know. Then I was mad with jealousy and now I am mad with grief. Perhaps it is all for the best. She won't be with him anymore, and it doesn't much matter what happens to me," Huber told one of the newsmen.

While at the jail, Huber was considered a model prisoner and was given the position of head hall man, an honor reserved for prisoners who were exceptionally well behaved. In July 1903, he was indicted for the murder of his wife and attempted murder of Fearing. Six months later, he agreed to plead guilty to second-degree murder.

Fearing was also a talkative chap when it came to the press. He told reporters that Gertrude had led him to believe she was free to see him since her marriage to Huber had been a sham without any legal documents to legitimize the union. Fearing also felt it was acceptable to fraternize with Gertrude since he believed Huber was a bigamist. It should be noted that Huber, while never producing the divorce papers from his first marriage, did provide the court with a marriage certificate proving he was Gertrude's husband.

About six weeks after his arrest, Fearing's father was able to furnish the $1,000 bail (more than $25,000 today) that had been set in the case, and the young man was released. His time in jail must have had quite an effect on Fearing, as he immediately quit the stage and became a traveling salesman. While free for the time being, he must have known that he could be facing more jail time for sleeping with a married woman. Fearing must have been kicking himself for his self-made troubles. The only reason he agreed to take Gertrude to Massachusetts in the first place was because she threatened to commit suicide if he didn't.

On January 11, 1904, Huber was brought to the Berkshire Superior Court to plead guilty to his crime. He sat next to Sheriff Charles Fuller, while his two defense attorneys, William Turtle of Pittsfield and the Great Barrington–based lawyer Charles Giddings, chatted with District Attorney John Noxon about the case. The prisoner wore a black suit, a white dress shirt and collar (this was a time when a collar and dress shirt were two separate items) and a black tie.

Huber's change of plea came as no surprise to those in the know, including an *Evening Eagle* reporter who told his readers "it has been predicted by the newspapers for months that the case would never be fought out in the courts. Huber has always had the sympathy of the public in connection with the shooting. He was completely wrapped up in his wife, and her actions apparently drove him almost crazy. That he did not plan to shoot his wife is generally believed."

The reporter's supposition stands in stark contrast to the fact that Huber told Gertrude's father he was going to kill her and then traveled from New York City to Monterey to do just that.

When the clerk called his name, Huber stood up and, in a clear voice, pleaded guilty to second-degree murder. Ten minutes later, he was being taken back to jail until his sentencing the following week. There was no doubt how that would end, since life in prison was the only sentence the law allowed for that particular crime.

Ten days after pleading guilty to murder, Huber appeared for sentencing before Judge Lloyd White. Huber's lawyers were late, and Huber agreed to be sentenced without his lawyers being present.

"I'm ready to be sentenced now," he told the judge.

White ordered Huber to serve a term of life in prison at the state penitentiary in Charlestown, but it would be a much shorter stay than Huber anticipated.

The same day Huber pleaded guilty and was sentenced to life in prison, Fearing also appeared in court and pleaded guilty to the crime of "fornication." Yes, there was, and is, such a crime in the Bay State. Fearing's attorney, C.H. Wright (who later became district attorney), argued that his client had already spent more than a month in jail unable to make bail as his father, the treasurer of an export lumber company that went into bankruptcy, didn't have the money readily available.

The plea fell on deaf ears, and Judge White sentenced Fearing to an additional sixty days in jail at the request of the district attorney.

Six years after Huber was sentenced to life in prison, Governor Ebenezer Sumner Draper pardoned him through the efforts of a number of prominent Berkshire County citizens, including Massachusetts state senator William Turtle, who, before turning to politics, was one of the two lawyers who represented Huber at trial; Charles Giddings, who was also involved in the move to free Huber; John Noxon, who had prosecuted the case as the district attorney; Senator Allen Treadway of Stockbridge, who was then senate president; and John Cleary, who was a reporter for the *Berkshire Courier* at the time of the murder and later rose to the editorship of a large New Jersey newspaper.

They believed, based on "a careful study of the case," that Huber had reformed while in prison and had "suffered enough." This was an era when killing your wife for cheating on you clearly wasn't considered the most heinous of acts. It had only been about thirty years since most states had begun to consider wife-beating a crime, and women's right to vote, or even sit on a jury in most states, was still years away.

While these learned men were obviously not forward thinking, Cleary's behavior went beyond the pale. He showed up at the Brooklyn candy store of Gertrude's parents.

"Don't you think Huber has been punished enough?" Cleary asked the old couple, who still struggled to make sense of the murder of their only child eight years after that tragic event. He waved a petition seeking Huber's pardon under their noses and tried to get them to sign.

"We're alone now and cannot forget the daughter we've lost," Rentel angrily told the newspaper editor in his thick German accent. "We will never feel kindly enough toward Huber to intercede for him. We are both alone now and cannot forgive him for making us so."

Their protests were in vain. On December 22, 1910, Huber received an unexpected visit from General B.F. Bridges, the prison's warden, who had official papers from the governor in his hand. Governor Draper and the executive council had decided the circumstances of Huber's crime were "of the most extenuating" character and that the shooting had been accidental. The idea that the murder was anything close to an accident is ridiculous and doesn't even jibe with what Huber told reporters just after the shooting or with any of the facts of the case, for that matter. Nonetheless, mostly thanks to the machinations of the aforementioned Pittsfield lawyers, Huber was about to be set free. Draper had originally refused to pardon Huber, but after losing the election, he went ahead and signed the paperwork two weeks before his term ended.

"Huber, you have been pardoned," Bridges told the shocked prisoner. "Now go get into your clothes and come down."

Huber was overcome briefly and took some time gathering the meager belongings he had collected in the six years he had been at the prison. He finally came downstairs with a small bundle under his arm and a dazed smile on his face.

"Glad to leave?" asked the warden, perhaps the dumbest question ever posed to a prisoner.

"Yes," responded Huber, grabbing the warden's hand and shaking it vigorously. "I'm going back to my mother for Christmas."

With a hearty thump on his back from Bridges, Huber was escorted out of Charlestown Prison. Outside the gate, he took his first breath of free air since he had murdered his wife on a warm fall day in Monterey eight years before. He immediately boarded a train for Brooklyn.

When Huber's aged mother, Amelia, learned of the news, she attempted to take public transportation to Grand Central Station to meet her son

Massachusetts governor Ebenezer Sumner Draper, who pardoned murderer George Huber in 1910. *Courtesy of the Library of Congress.*

but became lost and arrived after Huber had already come and gone. The heartbroken woman returned to the DeKalb Avenue home where she lived with a family who boarded her in return for cleaning the place. She slowly made her way to her room, where she found her son sitting on her bed waiting for her. A tearful reunion ensued.

The next day, they left the city for Trenton, New Jersey, where they spent Christmas with relatives. Meanwhile, the news had also reached the Rentels, and the rest of the neighborhood, especially the children who attended the school across from "Pop" and "Granny" Rentel's candy shop.

"Say, Pop," a boy asked as he purchased some penny candy and a Christmas card. "Did you have a daughter that was shot? What was her name?"

"Yes," Rentel answered. "We called her 'Trude.'" At this, his wife, sitting in the back of the shop, began to moan softly and mumble to herself in German. She had barely slept since receiving the news that her daughter's killer was free.

"*Solch ein Weihnachten!*" the old woman wailed, which was German for "such a Christmas." "It is much worse than to be dead. It is a strange country where a man can go free a few years after killing a young girl whom he lured from her home."

THE MURDER THAT NEVER WAS

J ohn Shufelt woke slowly from a deep sleep. It was just after midnight, and one of the children was crying out for a cup of water. He moved his arm across the bed to wake his wife, Esther, but her side was empty. He bolted upright, nervous since he knew his wife was prone to sleepwalking. He slipped his hand under her pillow, grasping for the scissors that she always kept there, a charm of sorts that Esther believed helped counteract her somnambulism, but they, too, were gone. John jumped out of bed and hurried from room to room. "Esther?" he began calling out, quietly at first, before becoming more frantic. He threw open the door and went outside, fearing that if his wife awoke outside in the darkness, she could lapse into a "fit," something she had dealt with since childhood after suffering a head injury in a fall.

He first looked for her near the house in North Egremont, Massachusetts, they rented on a desolate road about one and a half miles from town. Soon his search ranged farther afield. He stopped at the neighbor's place, but Esther wasn't there. Just after 1:00 a.m., he hurried by foot to Esther's father's home in Mount Washington, a number of miles away. The journey was useless, for Esther had not gone there either. Shufelt headed home nearly exhausted and no closer to an answer.

As he ranged through the rural countryside of southern Berkshire County on the night of May 8, 1879, calling out his wife's name, Shufelt had no idea he would soon be at the center of a police investigation into his wife's disappearance.

North Egremont, Massachusetts. *Photograph by author.*

In the following days, Shufelt took time off as a farmhand during the busy spring planting season to continue his search for Esther, but now, instead of fearing she had wandered off in a somnambulistic state, John was beginning to suspect she had left him for another man, sneaking out in the middle of the night and leaving her life and family behind. It was after his return home that first night that he began piecing his theory together. A thorough search of the house revealed four of Esther's dresses, her bonnet and other clothing and a black satchel were missing from the house.

The couple had had problems for several years since they married in 1870, when Esther was seventeen and John was twenty-three. He later alleged that he initially had doubts about marrying her since she had a reputation as being "fast" with the boys. But when she promised to mend her ways, the two were wed. By the winter of 1878–79, the relationship had begun to disintegrate. John would come home from a hard day in the fields to find several young men from the town hanging out at the house, and there was one in particular he despised. Henry Church was a trapper, fisherman and farmhand who had become close with Esther. She had apparently told friends she was thinking about running off with him. Shufelt claimed Church had two wives already and was a "bad man."

Shufelt learned that, on the day in question, Church had left town just hours before Esther disappeared. He began a fruitless search for the couple in Hinsdale and Richmond, two Massachusetts towns north of Egremont, and even into Spencertown in New York on what turned out to be spurious tips from gossipy folks around the county. He finally returned home and resumed his life as a field hand while attempting to juggle his children's needs, which eventually turned out to be too much for him. The children became wards of the town while Shufelt obsessed about tracking down his wife. He began to put money away in the hopes of scraping enough together to continue his search. He learned that Church had previously worked as a lumberman in Leyton, New York, near the Canadian border. Shufelt wasn't going to stop searching for his wife, he said, until he had "run her down."

Soon public opinion began to shift, and rumors that Shufelt had murdered his wife began to quickly spread, eventually making it into print in some of the local papers. Shufelt had been saying some odd things following Esther's disappearance, which began to throw suspicion his way. He allegedly told some local kids on their way to fish at Winchell Pond, near Shufelt's home, that they should be careful or they might "bring up something they did not wish to see." He was heard asking someone how long it would take a rope to rot in water if it was holding something down.

Deputy Sheriff Wallace Langdon of Great Barrington eventually began asking questions connected with Esther's disappearance. They were questions that seemed to indicate the lawman didn't believe the woman had run off with another man but rather that he thought her husband had done the woman in.

Langdon's investigation revealed there had been a mysterious man seen on the pond's edge who appeared to be searching the water for something—or someone—for three consecutive nights around May 8, and there was a track near the shore where a boat had been dragged across the grass. Shufelt's boat was searched but turned up no clues.

Rumors of physical abuse began to surface around this time. Neighbors told of how Shufelt would often beat Esther in jealous rages and once injured her so badly that the neighbors took her in and cared for her until she recovered. Locals told of how Esther, a plump and fresh-faced young girl when she first married Shufelt, had become a thin and haggard shell of a woman; they blamed Shufelt's treatment of Esther.

But the most damning evidence came from Shufelt's nine-year-old son, who claimed he witnessed his father murder his mother. According to the boy, that night, his parents quarreled and his father struck his mother in the head twice with a large piece of wood. After the second blow, his mother didn't speak again. The boy said he watched his father pick up the limp woman, throw her over his shoulder and leave the house. The boy said his father later returned to the house alone. Shufelt then threatened his son, telling him if he ever spoke about what happened, he would kill him. The boy later changed his story, telling the investigators Shufelt had offered him a bribe not to tell.

Shufelt told a very different story to the deputy of what happened on the night of May 8. On that night, Esther had wound the clock before bed as usual, then picked up their two-year-old and brought her into bed with her to keep the child from fussing. Their three other children were already tucked in for the night. Shufelt came to bed later, sliding over his wife and baby onto the side of the bed nearest the wall. He kissed his wife, turned toward the wall and fell asleep with the child between them. He woke to find his wife gone.

Langdon and some other officers from Great Barrington went to Shufelt's place and discovered what they believed to be bloodstains on the floor, plaster walls, a window sill and an area of wainscoting in the house.

Langdon didn't buy Shufelt's story, and in July, two months after Esther disappeared, he arrested Shufelt for murder. Officers, with the help of some local men, searched Winchell Pond, but no body was found. Even so, Langdon felt he had enough evidence to charge Shufelt, and the prisoner was brought to district court in Great Barrington. It was probably a good thing Shufelt was arrested because some of the hotheads in Egremont had contemplated lynching him.

A local reporter found Shufelt to be in good spirits, cheerful even, while awaiting his preliminary court hearing. Shufelt spoke at length about the case as he sat in jail in Pittsfield in cell seventy-three, which had become known as the "murderer's cell" due to its previous occupants. He gave the newspaperman a brief history of himself, telling him he had been raised in North Egremont and had lived in that area his whole life. The prisoner said he knew his case would be thrown out because his wife was alive and well and on the run with Church.

On July 18, 1880, Shufelt was hauled to the district court in Great Barrington for a preliminary hearing before Judge James Bradford to determine if he would be held for the grand jury. If the grand jury found there was enough evidence to indict him for first-degree murder, he would be heading to trial to fight for his life. Deputy Langdon had gathered upward of thirty witnesses for the hearing that morning. Shufelt sat next to his attorney,

Henry C. Joyner, while spectators, mostly from Egremont, and the press, including reporters from papers in Boston and Springfield, craned their necks in the small and tightly packed courtroom trying to get a look at the presumed killer. The crowd was looking forward to hearing the juicy details of the case, but they were soon disappointed.

Justin Dewey appeared for the District Attorney's (DA's) Office and, much to the relief of Shufelt and chagrin of the deputy, told the court he didn't believe there was enough evidence to charge the defendant with murder if the court required him to present the body of the victim.

"The only direct testimony we have bearing on this case is the testimony of the boy, a child of nine years old, and he appears to be of a weak mind," Dewey told the court. He went on to thank the officers for their hard work but said the state didn't have the money to dredge the pond looking for a body, and since the search for the woman outside the county hadn't turned up anything, they had done all they could and wouldn't go forward if the court required more proof. Dewey pointed out that there had been evidence that Shufelt had been abusive to his wife in the past and had even told people he wished she was dead and that no one had heard a peep from the woman since the day she went missing.

The judge chided the DA's Office for not putting enough effort into looking for the missing woman and told Dewey he "should have authorized the officers to make a thorough search."

Bradford then declared the child not competent to testify and discharged the prisoner. Shufelt was free, and a very lucky man, since the penalty for first-degree murder at the time was hanging.

The disappointed reporters, some of whom had traveled more than one hundred miles to be in court, were shown the infamous blood stains by the doctor who had examined them. He told them the stains were made by human blood and that one even had a piece of woman's hair stuck to it. The reporters were also allowed to question the star witness. The young boy would only tell them that he was afraid of his father and that his mother was dead.

SHUFELT WAS A FREE MAN, but the suspicion of having gotten away with murder clung to him like a stench he couldn't remove, making life in a small, rural town hard to bear.

It wasn't until nearly a year and a half after Esther went missing that Shufelt was finally vindicated. Deputy Sheriff Edwin Humphrey, an intrepid and dogged investigator, retraced Esther and Church's trek from Egremont to Albany, New York, to Mechanicsville, north of that state's capital. From there, the investigator took a skiff across the Erie Canal and made his way to Harts Falls, now known as Schaghticoke, where he learned that Esther and her new beau had briefly settled there but had already moved on.

A short time after the couple made their escape from Berkshire County, Church hired out Esther to a farmer from Harts Falls, Amos Bryant, but Bryant's wife suspected there was something suspicious about their new housekeeper and let her go a little more than a month after she started working for the family. Meanwhile, Church was working as a laborer for another farmer, Martin Haywood Jr. After Esther's discharge from the Bryant household, she too began working for the man. In August 1879, a month after Shufelt was brought to court, the couple gave away their old trunk, bought a new one and departed for parts unknown.

Humphrey returned to the Berkshires with the news and a fishing rod that had been left behind. The pole was identified as belonging to Shufelt and was considered proof positive that the man who once faced the gallows was indeed innocent of the murder of his wife.

It's unclear what happened to Esther Shufelt. Records indicate that Church was back in the area, without Esther, by 1900. Where Ester ended up remains a mystery.

Shufelt remarried in 1901. He married his second wife, Lillie Hoffman, in Hillsdale, New York, just across the border from Egremont. That marriage, while not as disastrous as the first, ended in divorce. A third marriage to a woman named Billie, close to twenty years his junior, fared better. They were still married when he died of an accidental shooting in 1917 while living in West Stockbridge.

THE RAILROAD MEN AXE MURDER

KILLING TIME

John Whalen was drunk on the night of August 29, 1891. He'd stumbled home from a night of drinking with his friend, co-worker and roommate, William Coy. Whalen, a thirty-year-old railroad worker, was passed out on his bed, still partially dressed. He never heard his friend slip into his room with the axe in his hand and was unaware Coy was now standing over him with the weapon raised above his head. The blade came down and smashed into Whalen's skull, and with another swing, the man's neck was split open, the blow severing the spine. Whalen was dead.

Now that Coy had just killed his roommate, next came moving the body. Removing the legs was hard work, but not as difficult as getting rid of the remains. It took Coy two trips to drag the body parts through a field that sloped up the side of Washington Mountain into a thick stand of young trees on an overgrown logging road that ascended steeply over decayed leaves, slippery stones, rotting tree trunks and rasping underbrush. One hundred yards past where the ragged logging road ended, about one and a half miles southwest of the train depot in the town of Washington, Massachusetts, he dug a shallow hole next to a rotten log and buried the remains.

After returning home, Coy did his best to get rid of the evidence, but he too was a little on the drunk side, and his cleanup wasn't perfect. Besides, he had other things on his mind. His wife had run off to Albany, New York, and

Above, left: William Coy. He murdered his friend and roommate, John Whalen, with an axe while the man slept. *Courtesy of the Library of Congress.*

Above, right: William Coy's victim, John Whalen. *Courtesy of the* Berkshire Eagle.

Left: Frances Coy, the wife of murderer William Coy and lover of his victim, John Whalen. *Courtesy of the* Berkshire Eagle.

he planned to bring her back home, even if home was a small, ramshackle affair that backed on to a hill.

The sun was up by this time, so Coy headed over to try to get his friend George Kelly, a redheaded lush who had an aversion to wearing shirts, to come help track down his wayward wife. Coy banged on the door, and Kelly's mother answered.

"Can I get breakfast? My wife's away," Coy asked the older woman. She let him in and fed him while Coy and her son chatted at the breakfast table.

Coy, who still seemed a little drunk, asked his friend to come with him and get his wife. Coy explained he'd learned where she had gone by pounding the information out of Whalen, who also happened to be a friend of Kelly.

"I can't afford to go," said Kelly.

Coy, pulling out a big wad of cash, responded, "I'll pay your way."

They returned to Coy's place and packed up some supplies while Coy explained in more detail about how his wife, Frances, had run off and was in New York State waiting for Whalen. Coy told Kelly that Whalen had met with an "accident" but offered no other details. The $30 (about $800 today) Coy gave Kelly helped curb any questions he might have had about the "accident." Kelly noticed his friend seemed to have plenty of money that day but didn't comment on the fact. They headed to the station and caught a train headed west toward Albany.

The Elopement

Frances had a two-day head start on her husband. She had left Friday night while Coy was out, most likely on a bender, and spent the night in nearby Becket before catching a train west. She and Whalen were supposed to meet on Monday in Albany, and from there, they would head to Kansas and begin a new life together. Whalen said he could secure a divorce for her, and the two would then marry. She was sick of living in a small shack with a drunken lout for a husband who left her alone most of the time while he went out and had his fun. She liked Whalen. He was sweet and, unlike her husband, soft spoken and even bought her presents. She and Whalen had hatched a plan to run off, and now it was actually coming true. Whalen was supposed to slip away with the trunk in which both their clothes and belongings had already been packed after he collected some money owed to him. They would meet at the train station on Monday.

With a little of the $50 (nearly $1,300 today) Whalen gave her, she got a room at the Globe Hotel, registered under a false name and waited impatiently for the time to come to meet her new beau. On Monday morning she woke up, breakfasted and then headed to the station, her heart racing at thoughts of her new life and their exciting journey. She was shocked not to find Whalen waiting for her. Instead, she found her drunken husband and his equally drunk friend Kelly. Frances was frightened, but Coy wasn't angry, he was downright sweet. He took her to a restaurant and then bought her a gold watch and new cloak and convinced her to come home.

By Monday afternoon, they were back at the little ramshackle house that Frances had hoped to escape for good. As soon as she stepped foot into the home, she began to suspect something bad had befallen Whalen. There were signs of a struggle in Whalen's bedroom, including two large blood spots on the wall, along with what appeared to be a bloodstain on a shirt left on the floor. The bed also had some disturbing clues. There was a smear of blood on the headboard and two large square pieces of material had been cut out of the mattress. A piece of the pillow and a hunk of the ratty rug on the bedroom floor had also been cut away.

Frances convinced their neighbor, Etna Geer, to let them stay with her.

"I can't sleep in my own house," she tearfully told her friend after showing her the various clues she had found. Coy remained mum about what, if anything, had happened while his wife was away. But for the two weeks they freeloaded at Etna's place, he drank heavily. When not in a drunken stupor, he was restless and appeared to be uneasy; he even made a point of wondering aloud where Whalen had gone.

The couple soon moved to Westfield, farther east into Massachusetts, where Coy secured a job as a streetcar driver. They left behind the torn-up mattress on a bloodstained bed in a room with a blood-smeared wall, all of which nearly shouted that something evil had taken place there.

SUSPICIONS

In the tiny town of Washington, it didn't take long for people to begin to gossip about the strange doings at the Coy residence and why Whalen had left so suddenly, and without his trunk, which was still sitting at Edna's place gathering dust. Another neighbor, Matilda Frost, soon began blabbing about hearing a row at the Coy place on the night Whalen was last seen. There was a lot of talk as well about how "a shiftless sort of farm laborer" and railroad worker like Coy had gotten his hands on the cash he was seen flashing around town just after his friend went missing. Finally, weeks after the murder, the selectmen of Washington notified the only state police investigator for the Western District—Detective Moses Pease, who resided in nearby Lee—about their concerns. Pease rode out with Deputy Sheriff Fred Cutting, also of Lee, to investigate. As soon as he entered the house, the detective suspected murder, even though he hadn't found a body yet, and rode into the town center to telegraph the chief of police in Westfield to arrest Coy.

Coy was hauled back to Berkshire County and arraigned the next day on a charge of murder. In the story Coy spun for Pease, he said he came home from Pittsfield to find the front door locked and the aforementioned signs of a struggle in Whalen's room. Coy walked to the train station to ask after his friend but was told he hadn't been by. Coy returned home and went to sleep. His explanation for having his friend's watch when arrested and where the money he had been throwing around the previous summer came from was that Whalen had admitted to Coy he "had been intimate" with his friend's wife and, in order to let the matter drop, had given Coy his watch and $100 ($2,600 today). This was the first of many versions of the story Coy spun.

Kelly was arrested the day of Coy's arraignment in West Springfield, Massachusetts, and was also charged with the murder of Whalen. Police thought he had possibly been involved in Whalen's killing or had at least helped haul Whalen's body onto Washington Mountain with his wagon and bury the remains. Kelly, during a jailhouse interview with local reporters, said he had gone over to Coy's house Sunday night to help him pack. "That's all I know about the case," he told the newsmen. Both suspects were remanded to jail without bail.

Around the time Coy was being arraigned, Town Selectman Alanson B. Pomeroy was out combing Washington Mountain looking for clues in the case when his dog, drawn by the rank smell of rotting flesh, made a beeline for a spot just off an old logging road. Pomeroy finally caught up with his pet, and when he pulled the mutt away from where the dog had been digging, he realized part of a man's suspender was visible. Upon closer inspection, he realized it was attached to something still partially buried in the ground. Pomeroy returned to town and telegraphed Pease.

Following Coy's arraignment, a reporter for the *Berkshire Evening Eagle* and another from the *Pittsfield Sun* rode out together from Pittsfield toward Hinsdale on the erroneous belief that was where the murder had taken place. Soon they were pointed in the right direction and arrived in Washington at the same time as Pease and Deputy Cutting, who were apparently not thrilled that the press had arrived. The whole group, led by Pomeroy and some other townsfolk, made the hike to the burial site.

A few minutes' work with some shovels and picks revealed Whalen's decomposing body or, to be exact, several separate parts of Whalen. The remains were located about eighteen inches under the ground. The body was doubled up, making a heap about four feet long and two and half feet wide. The stench that arose from the body was almost too much for the small crowd to bear.

Medical examiner Dr. Frank K. Paddock arrived that evening. The remains were taken out of the grave a short time later and carried to town, where Paddock examined them. Whalen's skull was crushed in, his throat was cut and both legs were cut off at the thighs. Whalen's body was turned over to his family in Becket a day after it had been found, and a short time later, he was given a proper burial.

When taken into custody, Coy seemed nonplussed to the point of appearing indifferent, possibly believing the body would never be found. When he learned that Whalen's remains had been discovered, his lips began to quiver and his entire body trembled violently. Between the evidence found at the house, the holes in Coy's story and the fact they had the body, the police felt they could make the murder charge stick, and Coy likely knew it as well.

INQUEST

The inquest into the case was held that Friday before Judge Joseph Tucker in Pittsfield. Kelly took the stand first. He recounted what he had already told reporters, as did Pomeroy (his dog, who actually discovered the body, was not questioned by the judge). The Coy's neighbor Mrs. Frost also took the stand and told how, just after midnight on the day of the murder, she heard a team of horses clatter by her house, heading away from the Coy place toward the old logging road. Inside the wagon, a dull light was thrown from a lantern that had been covered with a blanket. Someone walking behind the wagon also carried a lantern. When Frost next saw Coy, she asked him about it, and he admitted it had been him and that he had been out looking for Whalen.

A man by the name of Ransom Chase told the judge that he had seen Kelly after his return from Albany and that Kelly had bragged about Coy's deep pockets and the "hell of a good time" they had drinking in New York's capitol. Eliza Geer admitted to hearing a row at the Coy house and raised voices on the night of the killing. Kelly's mother told the court that her boy had been home Saturday night and therefore couldn't have been involved in the killing or burial.

The Coy's landlady in Westfield, Hoy Otis, was also called to testify and provided some damning evidence in the form of a suit of clothing that

Frances Coy had given to her. Frances told the woman Coy had bought the clothes in Albany when he was drunk and that they didn't fit. In truth, the clothes belonged to Whalen. The landlady also provided the police with a coat that appeared to be bloodstained, two hammers and a bottle with Whalen's initials on it. Otis told the court that Frances gave her the coat, and they discussed ways of trying to remove the stains. Otis also talked about the other items she had found under the Coys' bed when she was snooping around.

Meanwhile, Pease was hard at work on the case and had managed to recover the murder weapon at Coy's brother's place in Washington. Neither Coy nor anyone else, apparently, had gotten around to cleaning the axe, which was still stained with blood.

Pease had also learned that Whalen was originally from Becket, was a station hand for the Boston & Albany Railroad where Coy had been working and had lived with the Coys', paying $3.50 a week for room and board. On the day Whalen went missing, he had gone to Lee to collect a $100 debt and stopped at the train station and collected $100 in pay. With close to $300 (around $7,800 today) in his pocket, he met Coy in Pittsfield and then went to Westfield, Hampden County, where they spent a good part of the day together drinking. The two men returned to the Berkshires by train. While Coy went on to Pittsfield, Whalen disembarked at Washington and walked down the quiet country road toward the Coys' place. It was the last time he was seen until his remains were taken from their resting place on the mountain.

The investigators believed that Coy had planned the murder and that it had nothing to do with jealousy and everything to do with robbery. They surmised that Coy convinced Whalen to go to Westfield after they had already been drinking in Pittsfield in order to get him as inebriated as possible before killing him. They also believed Frances may have been in on the plan. Pease and Deputy Crosby kept working on Coy, and the prisoner told them a number of stories, altering the facts as the lawmen poked holes in each successive story.

In one version, Coy said he had come home Saturday night to find Whalen's room in the state police had found it, with blood on the walls and the carpet cut. After finding a chicken in a pot in the kitchen, he assumed Whalen had slaughtered the bird in his room. Coy's next story involved an old man named Flanghton whom Coy said had killed Whalen because of a grudge he had against the younger man. In another variant, the prisoner said he knew who had done the deed but had been threatened with death if he told. Coy's various versions of events continued to circle the truth until, a little more than a week after his arrest, with the police continuing to chip away at Coy's story, he finally cracked and confessed to the killing but claimed it was done in self-defense. His recounting of the details of the murder to the lawmen smacked of braggadocio and was told without a hint of remorse.

In this version, Coy got home around midnight and found the house deserted. He went out looking for Whalen, but having no luck, he returned home and found his roommate's trunk in the middle of the room. He ascertained that Whalen and his wife had plans to run away, so he decided to have a look at the luggage. He opened it and found his wife's clothing mixed with Whalen's things. As he was digging through the trunk, Whalen walked in.

"What in hell are you looking in my trunk for?" Whalen shouted at Coy, according to the prisoner. A quarrel ensued, and Whalen pulled an axe and a club out and swung the bladed weapon at his former friend, shouting, "Damn you, I'll kill you anyway and get back my hundred dollars!" (This was the amount Coy alleged Whalen gave him as recompense for having his way with Coy's wife.)

Coy said he caught the axe's handle as Whalen swung it at him—not once but twice—and wrenched it away from him. Whalen then grabbed the club and again came in for an attack, but Coy brained him with the butt end of the axe, killing him instantly.

Whalen had fallen onto his bed during his death throes, and as he lay there, Coy sat down to think about his options. After an hour of contemplation, Coy got up and took the axe to Whalen's throat to make sure he was dead before dragging the body outside. He then returned to Whalen's room, where he cut up the part of the rug, along with the pillow and mattress, which had bloodstains on them, and burned them. He never explained why he took such care with these details but didn't bother to clean off the blood splatter on the walls and the bed, although it was surmised he was drunk at the time, so maybe that had something to do with it. Coy then went back outside, chopped off his friend's legs and dragged the torso and then the legs up into the woods.

There were still numerous holes in the story. For instance, Whalen's head wound was located behind his left ear. Coy couldn't have possibly hit him there if the two were facing each other during the struggle as Coy contended. Needless to say, no one believed that version either, but with Coy's admission to the killing and various other pieces of evidence, Pease felt he had an airtight case.

A week after his confession, Coy asked to speak with Detective Pease and agreed to take him to where he had hidden the clothes Whalen had been wearing when he was killed. Under heavy guard, Coy walked back up the logging road for the first time since burying his former friend, but after they reached the turnoff to the burial site, Coy headed in the opposite direction, splashed through a little mountain stream to the opposite bank where a large rock stood and began to dig in the mud. He soon pulled up a coat and vest that were covered with mud and dotted with mildew; this hid any potential bloodstains at the time of the initial inspection, but the clothes later turned out to be covered in blood. On the way back to jail, the party stopped at the scene of the murder, and Coy once again gave a recitation of his (latest) version of the killing. While Coy tried to project some bluster as he pantomimed exactly how the struggle had taken place, his pale, clammy face; nervous hands; and uncontrollable shaking belied his boastful and expletive-filled recitation of the deed.

Court

As you might expect, the murder was the main topic of conversation in the Berkshires, from North Adams to South Egremont, and as every new tidbit of information—whether factual or not—came to light, tongues wagged anew. There were rumors that Coy had a third accomplice besides Kelly, but that turned out to be just gossip. The tenor of the talk was that Coy was as guilty as they come.

"The feeling of horror which filled the minds of the public when the particulars of the awful crime were brought to light, has in no sense lessened, and it is the general opinion that William Coy is guilty of deliberate murder," wrote one newspaperman.

Sitting in jail as his case moved through the court system, Coy was visibly nervous and exuded a sense of restlessness. His eyes darted back and forth as he sat in his cell, never focusing on a single spot for long, and his hands were like two birds flitting around until they briefly clasped one another; this process was repeated over and over, as if mimicking the thoughts of being hanged racing through his mind. Frances believed Coy would commit suicide if the chance arose and told the sheriff as much. The jailers kept a close watch on their charge to make sure he didn't try to cheat the hangman. Two small sharpened pieces of metal that could have been used to open a vein were found hidden on him, but he said he used them to cut his tobacco and not as a weapon. At some point as he and Kelly were being held at the jail, Coy was able to slip into his friend's cell. He begged Kelly to tell the police that he had witnessed Whalen threaten to kill Coy.

At Coy and Kelly's preliminary hearing in district court in Pittsfield, a massive crowd of curious residents and a contingent of reporters waited to get a glimpse of the now-infamous killer and his alleged partner in crime. Soon a closed carriage rumbled up Wendell Avenue and stopped near the courthouse. The prisoners, handcuffed to one another, were brought out by Detective Pease and Deputy Cutting and marched into the building as a crowd of several hundred people pressed in toward them to get a better look. Coy was dressed in a dark suit with a white shirt, but with a handkerchief pinned to the shirt in place of a collar (this was a time when a dress shirt and collar came separately, and apparently, Coy didn't have one available). His jet-black hair was shiny with oil and done up in a dandified style to match his equally dandified curled mustache. As hard as he tried to look stolid as he was being walked into court, his nervousness shone through. Kelly, on the other hand, didn't appear nervous at all and sat in the dock, his large arms casually folded across his chest, waiting for the case to start. He even wore a shirt, although he too was without a collar. The crowd kept growing in size, and the folks who couldn't fit inside the courtroom gawked at the scene through the room's various windows. Frances was also in court and sat quietly near the door, tears running down her cheeks. Whether this was for her husband's situation or for the loss of her lover is hard to say. Coy sat with his head in his hands through much of the testimony.

At the end of the hearing, the judge ordered that Coy continue to be held without bail for grand jury proceedings. Because no evidence was offered against Kelly (it appears he hadn't been involved in the murder after all), he was discharged by the court but was placed under bond to appear as a prosecution witness in the case. The lawmen and their prisoner had to fight their way through a massive crowd in order to get back in the carriage and return to the jail.

The following January, Coy was indicted for first-degree murder. On a bright and sunny Monday, March 21, 1892, he was put on trial for his life. The event was even better attended than Coy's earlier appearance in district court, and there was nary a space that wasn't filled with the curious, including a number of women and children. The onlookers craned their necks to get a look at Coy, dressed as he had been at his last court appearance, as he sat nervously chewing tobacco. The crowd quieted down when the three judges (yes, this trial featured three) entered the courtroom with great solemnity. Chief Justice Albert Mason entered first, followed by Judges John Hammond and Emory Aldrich. The chief justice sat in the central position on the bench with the other judges seated to left and right, respectively.

After an invocation by Reverend W.W. Newton, jury selection began. The lawyers went through nearly eighty men before getting a seated jury, as many of the county residents had already formed opinions about Coy's guilt.

One of the potential jurors told the court he had read the newspaper accounts but didn't take stock in what was written. To this comment, one reporter questioned the man's intelligence, writing "as he takes no stock in newspaper accounts he cannot of course take any apparent offense at this reflection of his intelligence."

District Attorney (and former Pittsfield mayor) Charles Hibbard gave a slow and methodical hour-and-a-half-long opening statement to the jury. It was evident to those in the audience that the prosecution had a very strong case against Coy. Hibbard, along with State Attorney General Albert Pillsbury, took turns questioning the many witnesses.

Among the various people called to the witness stand were Dr. Paddock, who conducted the autopsy, and several other learned men of science who all came to the same conclusion: Whalen had been lying down when he was struck with the axe. This being a very different time, the jury foreman was allowed to ask the doctor if the blow could have been made while the victim was standing. Paddock answered that he believed Whalen must have been lying down in bed when the axe blow was struck. Coy's defense attorneys, Herbert Joyner and C.J. Parkhurst, tried their best to mitigate the damage from this testimony since it was completely contradictory to their client's version of events, but it was an almost impossible task. Dr. Paddock also opined that the axe blow to Whalen's head, although a fatal wound, wouldn't have necessarily caused instant death, and he believed Whalen was still alive when his throat was cut by Coy. This too damaged the defense's case.

Kelly took the stand for the prosecution, but his testimony did little to help their case. On the first of two days of testimony, Kelly had a hard time getting through his story since he was drunk. On the second day, under cross-examination by the defense, Kelly spent much of the time denying he had, in fact, been drunk the day before while on the stand.

Kelly's testimony notwithstanding, minute by minute, witness by witness, the noose was slowly tightening around Coy's neck. His confession made it into evidence, as did the various bloodstained items from Whalen's bedroom, including the headboard. It wasn't looking good for the defense.

After the prosecution rested, Joyner asked the court to excuse the jury so he could discuss a matter out of their earshot. When the men left, he argued that the prosecution's evidence showed that Whalen hadn't been killed instantly by the axe blow to his head as the indictment had alleged, and because of this, no verdict could be rendered on the charges, and a new indictment was needed (if the judges agreed, the case would have to begin again). The attorney general argued that there was case law that showed the indictment didn't have to be that specific. The judges held off on making any decision at that point, and the trial continued. They would eventually deny Joyner's request.

On each successive day of trial, the crowds grew larger. At one point, the court security guards had to force the courtroom doors closed against the onrush of spectators and barred the way to prevent the surging crowd from pushing in.

In his opening statement, Joyner gave an eloquent and forceful speech in which he described the various forms of homicide:

> *Mr. Coy's crime was nothing more than manslaughter. There's no contemplation as to the killing. John Whalen came to his death by the hand of William Coy. Under what condition and provocation did William Coy kill John Whalen? Was the provocation such as to reduce the crime to manslaughter or to make it an excusable homicide? He relies on your good judgment whether this was an excusable homicide or such a homicide as the government claims it to be.*

Joyner told of how, as a child, Coy was stricken with an illness that left him partially deaf and with a frail body. The attorney focused on his client's lack of education and the extreme mental anguish he felt over the betrayal of his wife and best friend. He denied the killing was over money and went on to describe Coy's version of events.

The defense began by calling several witnesses who claimed Coy had been flashing his money around before the killing, which would negate the prosecution's allegations of robbery. Next came Coy's wife, Frances, whose testimony elicited murmurs from the gallery. She told the jury she was originally from Feeding Hills, near Springfield, Massachusetts, and that her maiden name was Veits. She had been married once before to a man named Myron Bates. She claimed she had been fourteen or fifteen at the time of her first marriage, but records indicate she was eighteen. She had been divorced for a year or two when, in May 1889, she married Coy. (She lied on the marriage license, indicating that she had never been married before.) She then described how she and Whalen had planned to run away to Kansas. Frances denied having been "intimate" with Whalen or even having kissed him. She likewise denied that she knew about or was somehow involved in Whalen's death.

After his wife's testimony, Coy took the stand in his own defense. He was nervous but managed to hold himself together through the testimony. Many in the crowd thought he did a fair job on the stand. He repeated the story he had told the police, with a few minor differences in detail, and adamantly denied that Whalen had been asleep in bed when he killed him.

In a move that shocked onlookers, the attorney general, obviously confident his case was rock solid, declined to cross-examine Coy. He relied on several rebuttal witnesses and a strong closing argument to help put the nails in Coy's coffin.

The defense gave its closing argument first. Parkhurst, who had a bit of a folksy air, began by telling the jury the case had been rushed through the system, making it difficult for "a country lawyer" to adequately prepare a defense against the attorney general of the state and his "able associate," the district attorney.

Parkhurst focused on the ideas of premeditation and "malice aforethought," elements required for a first-degree murder conviction. If he could convince the jury that Coy acted in the heat of the moment, he would be able to save him from the gallows. "What is manslaughter? It is an offense just below murder. Manslaughter requires that the mind should be clouded by passion which exerts the reason and destroys the judgement," the lawyer told the jury.

Attorney General Pillsbury then gave his closing statement, focusing on Coy's version of events and poking hole after hole in the defendant's story.

"The theory of self defense is impossible in view of the circumstances when they last met, in view of the condition in which Whalen went to his home; impossible in view of the subsequent conduct of the prisoner," he said. "Every word was a lie and every move a concealment."

Pillsbury tried to implicate Frances in the crime, suggesting she was in on the plan to murder Whalen. He said either she convinced Whalen to run away with her as a ruse to get him to collect a large sum of money so her husband could kill and rob him or that she made the elopement up after the murder in order to cover the true motive of the crime. This was, perhaps, disingenuous on the part of the prosecutor since, if they truly believed she had been in on it, they would have at least brought charges of accessory.

They certainly had no compunctions about charging Kelly with murder on flimsy evidence.

In another unheard-of procedure in today's world, Coy was allowed to speak directly to the jury before the judge elucidated the particulars of the law and they began deliberations.

"I've told you the truth. This thing was all caused by his being with my wife," he told the men who held his life in their hands.

After six long days of trial, the jury was out less than two hours on that Saturday, May 26, 1892. After giving a note to the judge through a court security officer indicating they had a verdict, the various parties were assembled, and the twelve men solemnly entered the courtroom and took their seats.

"Gentlemen of the jury, have you agreed upon a verdict?" asked the court clerk.

"We have," answered the jury foreman.

"Mister foreman look upon the prisoner. Prisoner, look upon the foreman. What say you, mister foreman, is William Coy, the prisoner at the bar, guilty or not guilty?" the clerk intoned.

"Guilty," the man answered. "Guilty of murder in the first degree."

It would be the noose for William Coy. He gazed intently at the foreman and then collapsed back into his seat. He paled considerably as the blood drained from his face. It was Coy's only show of emotion.

Coy's lawyers kept fighting for him even after the trial ended and the sheriff's office began building the scaffold they would use to execute the prisoner. The lawyers were able to stretch their client's time on Earth for nearly a year longer, but with each small victory and resulting defeat, Coy's emotional state roller-coastered from joy to anguish. He spent his time giving interviews in which he lashed out at the prosecution's witnesses, from Kelly to his old neighbor who had taken them in, Etna Geer, suggesting both knew more about the killing than they had let on.

"This whole thing is a fraud and a perjury," he told a reporter. "If those witnesses had told the truth about me, I wouldn't be here now."

EXECUTION

After nearly a year, Coy's luck finally ran out. His attorneys had done all they could, and his date of execution was set for March 3, 1893. The day before he was to die, he woke up from a restless sleep, ate little and seemed nervous and irritable. Outside, curious members of the public came to look at the newly built scaffold with the imposing noose that swung in the stiff breeze. Reverends John Clymer and Newton, who had given the invocation at the start of Coy's trial, visited him several times over the course of the day and remained with him overnight. Coy's sister also visited. In the afternoon, Coy and his sister spent an hour together, walking around the scaffold where, in less than twenty-four hours, Coy would be put to death. They both wept as they talked of the past and of their family. That night, a storm kicked up. The wind howled outside, and the snow pelted the windows while Coy attempted to sleep.

The next morning, Reverend Newton said a prayer for the doomed man, and then two deputies pinioned the prisoner's arms behind his back and cuffed him. The slow procession of men made its way to the gallows. When a deputy slipped the noose over Coy's neck and positioned the black hood on his head, the prisoner nearly collapsed and had to be held up. The reverend then spoke in a clear, loud voice. "William Coy desires me to say that he has given his heart to God and asks for mercy and forgiveness for his crime. He forgives all who have spoken against him and goes hence with charity for all and malice toward none."

There were about fifty people invited to the hanging, including a number of the jurors whose decision had led to this moment. They slid the hood down over Coy's face as Sheriff John Crosby, his voice trembling slightly, said, "In obedience to the command contained in the warrant, I now proceed to execute the extreme penalty of the law upon the body of William Coy by hanging him by the neck until he be dead. And may God have mercy on his soul."

At 10:43 a.m., after the pegs were pulled from the trapdoor, Crosby pressed the spring that released the trap and "launched Coy into eternity" in the words of an *Eagle* reporter who witnessed the execution. Coy's legs convulsed for a few seconds before going limp, his body swinging from the end of the rope for nearly six minutes before the doctor announced that no pulse was found. Sixteen minutes after the execution began, Coy's body was cut down from the rope.

Coy was the last man to both be hanged and the last to be executed in Berkshire County, as the state soon after introduced the electric chair for the job and centralized executions. To the very end, he maintained that he had killed Whalen in self-defense.

Part II

LESSONS IN TEMPERANCE

The old Adams, Massachusetts police station. *Courtesy of the Library of Congress.*

THE THANKSGIVING DAY DOUBLE MURDER

John Ten Eyck sat in jail in Pittsfield awaiting trial for a double murder. To help pass the agonizing hours before he would face a jury and possibly the end of a rope, he put pen to paper to tell his story in his own words and to "show the world how an innocent man may be slandered, and perhaps tried and convicted, condemned—perhaps executed—through prejudice grown out of false reports and without the slightest foundation."

It was 1878, and Ten Eyck, a black farm laborer, carriage driver, cabinet maker and itinerant woodcutter was heading to trial on somewhat flimsy circumstantial evidence for the murders of David Stillman and his wife, Sarah, an elderly couple who owned a prosperous farm in Sheffield.

On the night of Thanksgiving 1877, just after 5:00 p.m., as a light snow began falling, Ten Eyck stopped fifteen-year-old John Carey Jr. on the road that led to the farm. Carey worked for the Stillmans doing farm chores, including milking the cows. Ten Eyck inquired whether the Stillmans sold butter and if they had any guests that night.

"Go and see if they have butter or company," he told Ten Eyck. "They're in the habit of selling butter."

Ten Eyck thanked him for the information and headed south toward the Stillmans' farm. Other Sheffield residents saw Ten Eyck heading in the direction of the farm that evening as well.

Carey—the last person, besides the killer, to see the elderly couple alive—was also the person who discovered the murders the next morning. The scene he found was bloody beyond comprehension. One newspaper described the crime as "one of the most brutal human butcheries ever committed in New England." While this may have been mere hyperbole, the scene was indeed gruesome.

That morning at about 6:30 a.m., Carey went to the farm and began doing his chores in the barn without going inside the home. He fetched the milking pail and milked the cows as usual. Carey hauled the milk to the house, but as he entered, he noticed the door between the woodshed and kitchen was open, which was unusual. He dropped off the milk and stopped cold. David Stillman sat on the couch where Carey had last seen him, but something was wrong. Stillman was dressed as he had been the previous day, but his outfit was now drenched in blood from a massive head wound. There were blood smears leading to the cellar and a bloody handprint on the wall in the cellar stairwell. Carey ran for help.

James Roraback, a neighbor, entered the home and followed the blood trail leading down the cellar stairs where he discovered Sarah Stillman in the cellar, dead from several axe blows to the head. The coroner later testified that at least two of the wounds would have been instantly fatal.

Back upstairs, Roraback found a pitcher of cider smeared with blood and a bloody axe with hair stuck to it. A block of butter and a set of scales were found set out upstairs, as if the couple had been in the midst of a sale when the killings occurred. Trunks in the house seemed to have been rummaged through, but it appeared that nothing had been taken. The sheriff was called, and during the ensuing investigation, some half-burned matches were found in the home's garret, as if someone had tried to set a fire to cover their crimes but had failed.

It didn't take long for the investigation to focus on Ten Eyck. Roraback recalled a conversation from the previous summer in which Ten Eyck complained about Mrs. Stillman, a large, excitable woman, because she had yelled at Ten Eyck about bothering her for hard cider on one too many occasions. According to Roraback, Ten Eyck had said he would "fix" the old couple.

Casey, the farm hand, told investigators of the conversation he had with Ten Eyck the day before, and soon, a flood of other witnesses began to come forward, tightening the noose around Ten Eyck's neck. There was Charles Stone, the local pharmacist, who said Ten Eyck showed up at his store one Thursday night and bought brandy and hair dye—he had asked for the quick-acting type—and paid with a crisp new five dollar bill. Two villagers recalled that just the day before, Ten Eyck had said he was broke. Then there was the bloodstained cane Ten Eyck was seen cleaning by his "friend" Nat

Johnson. Ten Eyck had left the cane at the man's house on Thursday night. Several people also recalled the suspect borrowing matches from them that Thanksgiving Day.

The Sheffield police tracked Ten Eyck to the home of William Lyons. According to Lyons, Ten Eyck told him to lie and say he wasn't there. Lyons told police the suspect was inside. They went in and found Ten Eyck hiding behind a post "straight as a broom handle." Ten Eyck was hauled off to jail and held pending trial. On the way, he seemed shocked to learn why he had been arrested. When they arrived, there was an angry mob of more than two hundred people with lynching on their mind. The police and sheriff's deputies kept the crowd at bay, and the prisoner was safely brought inside and locked up.

Now sitting in jail in Pittsfield, he began to tell his story. Born in Lenox around 1832, he was the son of a local woman, Orrilla Mariah Fletcher, and John Ten Eyck, a former slave from New York who had escaped to Massachusetts.

John Ten Eyck's life started out rough. He had an absent father and a mother who abandoned him and his brother when Ten Eyck was only thirteen months old. The brothers were turned over to another couple to be cared for. The couple who raised the boys, Joseph and Nancy Kelson, were foster parents before such terms came into general use and had cared for other poor or orphaned children in Lenox for many years before the Ten Eyck boys came to stay with them. The Town of Lenox gave the couple financial support, the equivalent of a little more than fifty dollars a month to care for the children. Ten Eyck wrote that "Old Berkshire, my birthplace, makes the most limited provision" for the poor, less than any other place he lived. He said no other county could "match injustice and oppression of the poor."

When John was five, and his brother, William Henry, seven, Lenox officials decided to offer the children to local farmers as indentured servants until the boys turned twenty-one. But Nancy wouldn't hear of it. Rather than let the town farm the children out, the Kelsons moved from Lenox and sent the boys to school.

Over the ensuing years, Ten Eyck would spend his part of the year working, mostly for local farmers, and attend school in the winter. "I was always looked upon as an honest and trustworthy boy by all who knew me," he wrote.

At fourteen, while working for a Pittsfield lawyer, Ten Eyck had his first taste of liquor. It was Red Mary, an Irish cook who liked her rum and would often send Ten Eyck to fetch it for her, who gave him his first taste. She poured a little in a glass, sweetened it with sugar, spiced it with nutmeg and topped it off with hot water. Sitting in jail, he recalled that moment, the taste of the liquor as it went down and how he felt afterward. He wrote about the experience with what sounded like nostalgia, but with bitter regret as well.

"Oh! Cursed be that first glass," he wrote. "I warn all young men and boys never to yield to such a temptation, for I tell you of a truth, it has caused me worlds of trouble and sorrow."

Ten Eyck went back to school that winter, but come spring, when he had turned fifteen, his school days were done. He became an itinerant woodcutter and farmhand full time. He also began to drink more heavily.

Ten Eyck first married at age sixteen. His wife, Rebecca Robinson, was twenty. Their first child, a boy, died of whooping cough when he was only five months old. The next year, they had a daughter who also perished of disease as an infant. During this time, the couple bounced around the county, going where the work was. For at least part of the time, the couple lived apart, as Rebecca worked as a housekeeper, which had the advantage of room and board.

Their third child, who also died in infancy, was the catalyst for the couple's permanent break-up. Ten Eyck said the baby was white, which "put a damper" on him, since both he and his wife were black.

"I now resolved that I would let her take care of herself and all the white babies she had in mind to have, and so we parted," he wrote.

Ten Eyck married again a few years later and moved to Blandford, Massachusetts, east of Berkshire County, where he had a job chopping wood. The only problem was that he had failed to divorce his first wife, something the papers would later latch onto to show how base and depraved Ten Eyck was. The newsmen also keyed into Ten Eyck's arrest record. He served three years of hard labor for forging a check from one of his employers. According to Ten Eyck, the man had cheated him out of part of his pay for showing up late for work on several occasions, and that was his way of getting the money he was owed and then some. He added a one in front of the ten on the check. He said he paid back the money before the case went to trial, but the judge sent him to jail anyway. Ten Eyck went on to note that besides that crime, he was innocent of the others he had been charged. He did six months in jail after a farmer accused him of stealing a bag of meal, but at the time of the alleged theft, Ten Eyck had been in jail on the forgery charge. He was drunk at the trial and didn't bother to defend himself. The townspeople of Hinsdale, Massachusetts, got up a petition to get Ten Eyck out of jail for the false charges, but by the time it made it to the governor, he only had two weeks left of his sentence and finished it out.

Ten Eyck had a boy and a girl with his second wife, both of whom lived to adulthood. His wife ran off with another man, and the children were raised by their grandmother in Blandford. He married a third time, again without bothering to divorce the other women. He would also eventually confess to setting fire to the barn of General Edward Phelps in Colebrook, Connecticut, as well as to the burglary of Judge John Sedgwick's home in Norfolk, Massachusetts. Sedgwick had been a New York State Supreme Court justice before retiring to Connecticut.

Ten Eyck, in his memoir, goes into great detail about his early days, including a list of every teacher he ever had during his years of schooling. But he ends his life story short of the day in which the couple was killed. While proclaiming his innocence, he avoids any mention of the facts of the case, thus failing to provide proof that he wasn't the perpetrator. He tells his readers that although some people may think him guilty of the murders and that he was only writing the sketch of his life because he feared being convicted, he claims not to have any doubt that he would be acquitted and swears "before God and man…I am an innocent man." He said he wrote the sketch—which he knew wouldn't be published until after his trial—only to let the public know "I am not as bad a man as the papers have represented me to be."

His lawyer also failed in proving his client's innocence but put up a solid defense against the charges. The trial in Pittsfield began on May 15, 1878, and lasted four days. An all-white jury of twelve men were quickly assembled, and the proceedings began with a forty-minute opening statement by District Attorney Nehemiah A. Leonard followed by the witnesses for the prosecution, including the coroner, who described the victims' wounds in gruesome detail, and a string of witnesses, including neighbors, lawmen and Ten Eyck's former friends who all pointed the finger at the defendant.

The trial saw a surprise witness take the stand for the prosecution, Ten Eyck's brother, William Henry. When Ten Eyck was arrested, police found $10.90 on him. He initially told the officers that he had saved up the money but then changed his story, insisting his brother, William Henry, had sent it to him in order to buy butter. Ten Eyck had tried to smuggle out a letter while in jail purported to have been written by his brother that stated William Henry had been barred from visiting the defendant and that he had indeed sent money to his brother. William Henry, who came from New Haven, Connecticut, took the stand and denied he had sent his brother money or

THE LIFE

OF

JOHN TEN EYCK,

WRITTEN BY HIMSELF, WHILE IN PRISON AWAITING TRIAL FOR THE
MURDER OF MR. AND MRS. DAVID STILLMAN,
OF SHEFFIELD, MASS.

ALSO A FULL REPORT OF THE TRIAL, CHARGE TO THE JURY,
AND VERDICT, WITH A SKETCH OF THE PLACE WHERE
THE CRIME WAS COMMITTED.

PUBLISHED BY

DAVID O'CONNELL.

PITTSFIELD, MASS.
SUN BOOK AND JOB PRINTING ROOMS, 16 1-2 NORTH STREET.
1878.

The cover page from John Ten Eyck's autobiography. *Public Domain.*

that he had ever written a letter to that effect. It was the final nail in Ten Eyck's coffin.

David O'Connell, the man who was busy helping to write Ten Eyck's life story, also took the stand and told of how the defendant had passed him the letter and told him to give it to his lawyer. Perhaps O'Connell believed he was doing the right thing by testifying, or maybe he had a more pecuniary reason for his actions, since a book about a convicted criminal would certainly sell better than one about an acquitted man. Either way, his testimony also helped seal the prisoner's fate.

Ten Eyck's lead attorney, Herbert Joyner, tried his best to stanch the flow of evidence against his client. He told the jury that this was a "double tragedy" in that the police and public, based on skimpy circumstantial evidence, immediately blamed Ten Eyck for the crime instead of following up on other leads and potential suspects. He mentioned a murder from around the same time committed by a tramp and discussed the fact that there were always vagabonds on the roads who were not above committing heinous crimes.

Joyner asked the jury whether it made sense that Ten Eyck, if he indeed planned to kill the old couple, would have been so blatant as to enquire from their farmhand whether they had guests that night or if he would have been so stupid as to saunter over to the pharmacy after the killings and ask for hair dye.

He picked apart the prosecution's witnesses, especially Ten Eyck's brother, who he said committed an "unnatural act" by testifying against his own kin.

The defendant took the stand in his own defense and stuck to his story about getting money from his brother. He said that he was at home at the time of the killing. He went to the drugstore and bought some hard cider and then went to a friend's house, where they drank until he fell asleep.

The jury spent only a few minutes deciding Ten Eyck's guilt. As soon as the members were in the jury room, they took a straw poll and found they all agreed he was guilty of the murders. They went ahead and skimmed some of the evidence and, a few minutes later, again took a vote. Guilty. To keep up appearances, they waited for a little over an hour before coming back with the verdicts.

The courtroom was deathly silent as the twelve men filed in. D.C. Smith, a Dalton resident, stared straight at the defendant when pronouncing the guilty verdicts. Ten Eyck showed no emotion.

Before being sentenced, Ten Eyck stood before the judge and told him he was innocent.

"They are the facts and as I also told the jury nothing but the truth in any form, that is all I have to say, sir. "

Judge James D. Colt, his voice trembling, told the defendant he had committed "the most appalling crime," one of "greater magnitude than ever committed in the county before."

The judge told Ten Eyck to turn his thoughts to God and beg for his forgiveness. As the sentence was read, everyone in the courtroom stood.

"[The] sentence is that you, John Ten Eyck, be taken from this place to the county's jail...and that on the 16th day of August next you be thence removed to the place of execution, there to be hung by your neck until you are dead. And may God in his infinite wisdom have mercy on your soul."

The night before he was to be hanged, Ten Eyck did not sleep. That morning, he methodically and quietly went about his ablutions. At 10:45 a.m. on August 16, 1878, he was escorted to the scaffold, and as 250 people looked on, he firmly and deliberately made his way up the stairs and stood on the trapdoor. Reverend Samuel Harrison, a black minister who had served with the famed Massachusetts Fifty-fourth Volunteer Infantry (Colored) a decade before during the Civil War, gave the man a final prayer. Ten Eyck refused to give a speech. The noose was slipped over his neck, followed by a black hood. The executioner pulled the lever, and Ten Eyck dropped. He died almost instantly.

His body was sent to his family in Blandford for burial, but in a final indignity to a man whose whole life had been filled with them, his father-in-law, from Ten Eyck's second marriage, exhibited Ten Eyck's body at ten cents a head in Chester, Massachusetts, at the Albany & Boston Railroad station. Ten Eyck's father-in-law made $350 that day before moving on to Blandford, where Ten Eyck was finally laid to rest. There were rumors his father-in-law later dug him up and sold his remains to a resurrectionist (body snatcher) for medical science.

6

THE CARD GAME KILLING

The Crime

They had been drinking together most of the day on November 1, 1878, when the cards came out. It was just a friendly game of poker. But at some point during the game, William Montgomery's thoughts began to fester. He'd supplied the booze, the cards, everything. Why shouldn't he ask for a little something from the other men to help with the outlay?

Montgomery stood up suddenly, went to the front door and locked it. His two friends didn't pay much attention to their drunken friend until he demanded a dime each for the cider they'd consumed, the equivalent of about $2.50 today. They thought he was joking until he began to get angry. He'd invited them over that day and was freely pouring the booze. Why should they have to pay? The situation quickly spiraled out of control.

To defuse the situation, Montgomery's wife came into the room, unlatched the front door and told her husband's friends to leave. Thomas Hall and George Ellis didn't need to be told twice. They knew Montgomery's temper. The men bolted for the door and were hurrying down the road when a shotgun blast split the night. Ellis dropped to the ground, his arm and side on fire. His moans replaced the roar of the gun. When Montgomery realized what he had done, his anger was replaced by dread and remorse.

The interior of a holding cell in the old Adams, Massachusetts police station. *Courtesy of the Library of Congress.*

THE PUNISHMENT

Montgomery sat in jail, held on $2,000 bail (nearly $50,000 today), while his friend lay in bed slowly dying. The thirty-year-old prisoner was a wreck. There were myriad conflicting stories concerning Ellis's prognosis, which meant the difference for Montgomery between aggravated assault and battery and murder, possibly first-degree murder, which carried only one punishment: hanging. He told reporters that it had all been a joke that went terribly wrong and that he had only asked the men for money to see if they would actually cough it up. When his wife opened the door, Montgomery grabbed his gun, telling his wife, "I'll fire into the air and scare 'em." He stepped to the door with the weapon at his side, but the shotgun discharged before he had a chance to raise it skyward. "I didn't see the boys when the gun discharged; I didn't aim at them, and was only intending to frighten them, just for a joke." He believed he would get off with no more than four or five years in prison if Ellis didn't die. Montgomery was a common laborer who was born in Williamstown and hadn't been in trouble with the law before, the prisoner told the reporter.

In the weeks since the shooting, the *North Adams Transcript* reported that Ellis was dying and then reversed itself, saying he was fine, had only been winged by the shot and that the cause of his "recent prostration was overeating on Thanksgiving Day." The paper then reported that, in fact, Ellis was dying from a loss of blood and had gotten gangrene in two of the fingers of the right arm, which had been hit by the blast. This later report was apparently the most accurate because on the night of December 26, 1878, Ellis died. An autopsy found twenty-six shotgun pellets in the victim's arm and that an artery had been perforated. It's a wonder Ellis managed to live for nearly two months. This was a time when blood transfusions were not commonly given. It was considered a dubious practice by the American medical establishment and was a dangerous procedure since no one knew there were different blood types. It doesn't appear Ellis received any transfusions as he lay in bed slowly bleeding to death.

Montgomery was now facing a murder charge and the possibility of hanging. When a reporter stopped by the killer's cell, he found Montgomery praying in the corner. When Montgomery finished, he came over and shook hands with the newsman. He was nervous, and there were tears in his eyes. He expressed profound regret for what he'd done. "I had hoped he would recover," he said. "I am sorry for his wife and family, and for him, also." The prisoner said although his wife and children hadn't come to see him in jail, they at least wrote to him on a regular basis. "It's awful lonesome here and I'd give anything to see my wife and children."

Montgomery planned to take the case to trial and explain to the jury that it had all been just an accident. "I know it will sound queer to you," he said, "but I put my trust in God." A few months later, he was shocked to learn he had been indicted for first-degree murder, having believed he would be charged with a lesser crime. He was now facing the gallows. His friends and

A contemporary view of downtown Adams, Massachusetts. *Photograph by author.*

family scraped up enough cash to hire attorney and former state senator Samuel W. Bowerman to represent him. Instead of taking the case to trial, under the advice of Bowerman, Montgomery took a deal and pleaded guilty to second-degree murder in April 1879 and was sentenced to life in prison a month later. But at least he didn't swing from the end of a rope.

THE BLOODSTAINED BADGE

THE DEED

The raised voice of Chief William F. Dinneen echoed through the North
Adams police station and could be heard downstairs by several of the
officers who were just getting off duty. It was a little after 6:00 p.m. on
Thursday, December 17, 1903. Dinneen was berating Patrolman Gardner
Northrup for showing up for duty drunk. Captain Frank Jones had already
told Northrup he would be suspended for his behavior, but the intoxicated
patrolman thought he could persuade the chief, whom he had known for a
few years before joining the force, to let him stay on.

"You are not in a condition to go upon the street in uniform. Your presence
there would be a disgrace to the city," the chief, who was a teetotaler, shouted
at Northrup. "You're a disgrace to the force. Go home."

Suddenly, the report of a pistol ripped through the station. A few seconds
later, there was another. Northrup had drunkenly fired his .32-caliber service
revolver twice, hitting his superior officer with one of the shots. The two
men were so close to one another that Dinneen's face was covered by the
gunpowder from the patrolman's pistol. The chief, as tough as they come,
was grazed in the abdomen by a bullet, but still managed to chase Northrup
down the hallway before Northrup again opened fire. The next shot was the
most serious, entering Dinneen's mouth and lodging in his throat.

After hearing the first shot, the men downstairs assumed someone had
accidentally discharged a weapon, but when the second report rang out,

Officers Henry Whipple and Patrick Walsh, already in their street clothes and about to leave after the day shift, rushed up the stairs toward the chief's office on the second floor. Whipple made it up the stairs first just in time to see Northrup dash from the hall into an adjoining lounge followed by the chief. A few seconds later, they were both back in the hall. Northup fired a fourth shot, which struck the chief's right hand when he threw it up in a protective gesture as he crouched near the ground. Whipple ran toward the two men, slid past the chief and tackled Northrup, but not before Northrup turned the gun on himself. He pointed it at his own chest and pulled the trigger, but the bullet missed its target and ended up only grazing his chest, near his heart. Whipple, slightly larger and stronger than Northrup, still had a hard time getting the pistol from his coworker's hand. As quickly as Northrup's violent behavior had begun, it subsided. His body went slack, and he stopped fighting.

"I'll go with you, Hen. Anywhere you say," he told Whipple, allowing himself to be taken to a holding cell. "I did it. I don't know why I did it. I must have been crazy."

Dinneen made it down the stairs and into the main office, blood pouring from his mouth and hand, his uniform soaked in it.

"I guess I'm done for," he said haltingly to the officers who had gathered there. "I have been shot, boys. I want you to understand why this man has shot me. He was drunk, and I wouldn't let him go on duty."

A horse-drawn ambulance arrived, and two doctors helped load the chief into the vehicle, which then rushed to the hospital. Once there, Dinneen's wounds were examined. The shot to his belly hadn't penetrated the abdominal cavity as originally feared, but the slug that had entered his mouth had split his upper lip, shattered several teeth, grazed the side of his tongue and lodged in the left side of his neck. The doctors were having a hard time locating the projectile in his neck and decided it was best to leave it there, believing it would be more dangerous to try to remove the slug. Dinneen's right hand had what's called "a through-and-through" wound, meaning the bullet had passed all the way through his hand, near the wrist. The hand had been crippled since youth, so the doctors weren't overly concerned about it. Before going into surgery, the chief made out his will and was visited by a Catholic priest who gave him his last rites. These two acts seem to have been done as a precaution, after all, it was a time before antibiotics, and many modern medical practices, such as aseptic surgery, were just starting to come into practice. As Dinneen lay on an operating table, back at the station, another bloody scene was playing out.

In the confusion of the harrowing scene, none of the officers had bothered to frisk Northrup before locking the forty-year-old up, and when two of his coworkers went to check on the prisoner, they found him covered in blood after having cut his own throat with a jack knife that he carried on him. The three-inch gash ran along the front of his neck and penetrated the flesh near the windpipe. The two doctors who were called to attend to Northrup found that the injury wasn't life threatening. He was treated for his wounds at the police station. The self-inflicted grazing wound to the chest was described as "merely a scratch" by local reporters. Not long after his suicide attempt, reporters were allowed to question Northrup, who seemed dazed and sometimes became incoherent during the questioning. He admitted what he had done and said he had no excuse for shooting the chief. He blamed Captain Jones for what happened.

"If the captain had let me go on duty there wouldn't have been any trouble," he told the reporters.

Word about the shocking incident spread quickly through the small city, and like the children's game of "telephone," as the story spread, it became twisted. Soon there were reports that both the chief and Northrup had been fatally wounded. In truth, by the next day, both men were out of any danger. The forty-year-old Dinneen was a physically resilient man. The six-footer weighed in at 210 pounds of muscle, not fat. It was reported that, to him, "fear was an unknown quantity." He had seen his fair share of altercations with local toughs over the course of his sixteen years on the job and during his prior service as a city marshal. Back when he was still a patrolman, nine years earlier, he had been beaten with a club by a member of an angry mob in Pownal, Vermont, when he and some other officers were investigating a case of liquor being sold to a minor. The officers put up a brave fight but barely escaped the frenzied locals. Afterward, Dinneen lay in a hospital bed for several weeks in and out of consciousness from a skull fracture. But he was tough and pulled through, rose through the ranks and became chief of police in 1899, at the age of forty.

It didn't take the news long to travel south to Pittsfield and the offices of the *Berkshire Evening Eagle*. A reporter was quickly dispatched to North Adams. Apparently, the man they sent wasn't much of a wordsmith and didn't feel he could do the scene justice because, he wrote, "the excitement that prevailed in North Adams after the shooting can better be imagined than described." While perhaps words failed the intrepid reporter in this instance, he got the point across: North Adams, and the rest of the Berkshires, were in shock and were wondering how this tragedy had come to pass.

Downtown North Adams in the early 1900s. *Courtesy of the Library of Congress.*

THE LEAD UP

A little before 6:00 p.m. that Thursday, Northrup stumbled into the station and prepared to start his overnight shift. When he passed Captain Frank Jones on his way to the locker room, Jones could smell the booze wafting from Northrup. He told the patrolman to go home, for he was in no condition to work.

Northrup had always been a reliable officer. A former butcher from Hoosick Falls, New York, he'd been on the force for about three years without any incidents, but of late, his drinking had become problematic, and he had been warned by his superiors to lay off the booze while on the job. Northrup may have deluded himself that he had his drinking under control, especially since he had escaped any official reprimand thus far, but his luck finally ran out. He had accrued a sizable amount of debt before moving to Massachusetts and was paying it off slowly. Dinneen was acting as the middleman between Northrup and his creditors. While this wasn't likely the reason for the shooting, in Northrup's alcohol-besotted mind, there may have been some deep-seated resentment against the chief linked with the embarrassment of the state of Northrup's finances, which helped ratchet up the exchange and pushed the officer past his breaking point.

Instead of leaving the station as the captain had ordered, a sulky Northrup went upstairs to the locker room. Sure, he had had a couple of drinks that afternoon, but he wasn't drunk. He was fully capable of going on duty, he thought, sitting down on a bench and beginning to stew. The officers of the day shift, including Whipple and Walsh, came upstairs to change into their civilian clothing and saw Northrup sitting there. Seeing he was in an unsociable mood, they cracked a few jokes without much response from him, changed out of their uniforms and headed downstairs to leave for the day. They thought little of their fellow officer's demeanor, as he was always a bit on the uncommunicative side. The rest of the night shift had already left the station to begin walking their beats. Northrup sat there a bit longer and then hauled himself up from where he sat and headed for the chief's office. Dinneen had already left his office and had been heading home for supper but had returned to the second floor to let someone speak to a prisoner who was being held in the lock-up. The chief was once again getting ready to leave when Northrup accosted him.

Northup later recalled that it was the captain he had wanted to shoot, but instead, he found himself trying to convince the chief, a man who didn't even imbibe, that he was sober enough to work. Northrup's anger rose as Dinneen continued to back the captain's decision and wouldn't be swayed by Northrup's pleas. Finally, his anger reached the boiling point. Northrup pulled his revolver and began firing.

THE MORNING AFTER

In the sober light of day, Northrup was full of regret, and his thirst for vengeance had dissipated. He asked about the chief and was relieved to hear it appeared Dinneen would make a full recovery. By the time Northrup woke that Friday morning, he had already been fired from the force by Mayor Frank Stafford.

Northrup thought about his wife and two young daughters and was distraught knowing what he had put them through because of his rash behavior and that it was only going to get worse from here. He was ready to take whatever punishment came his way. If the chief suddenly took a turn for the worse and succumbed to his wounds, Northrup would surely get the chair. His wife, Helen, came to see him that day, and although the exchange was not recorded for posterity, one can imagine the tearful scene that must have ensued.

That same morning, Dinneen's wife, Ellen, sat with her husband as he lay in a hospital bed. She had been by his side all night. Only a few weeks before, they had celebrated their sixth wedding anniversary, and now her husband was laid up, his face and neck horribly swollen from the gunshot he took to the mouth. He had just narrowly escaped death, but seemed to be in good spirits and was even able to relate the incident to the reporters who crowded around his hospital bed.

THE SENTENCE

Northrup was soon arraigned on a charge of assault with the intent to murder, but possibly due to his having been a police officer, he was released on bail. A little more than a month later, Dinneen had sufficiently recovered to appear before a grand jury and was able to describe what had happened. On January 22, 1904, Northrup was indicted and appeared in the Berkshire Superior Court in Pittsfield in order to plead guilty to the charge and throw himself on the mercy of the court, but mercy came from quite a different quarter.

The courtroom was thronged that day with every seat in the gallery filled. Northrup sat with his wife in the front row awaiting his turn before Judge Lloyd White. The case was called, and Northrup stepped up and took a seat beside his attorney, Mark Couch.

The defendant sat quietly listening to District Attorney John Noxon relate the details of his crime to the judge.

"The relations between the chief and this man Northrup had been friendly during the term while this man had been an officer there and what the exact state of mind of this man was at this time that could cause him to commit this murderous assault upon the chief is something that is hard to explain," the long-winded DA told the judge. "The chief of police is here, and perhaps your honor would like to hear what the chief knows with reference to this case and to the state of feeling between the two men prior to this time."

Judge White did indeed want to hear from Dinneen. There were murmurs from the crowd as the chief stood up and moved closer to the judge's bench. Noxon and the judge questioned the chief about the incident and were told that there had never been any trouble between himself and Northrup prior to the shooting.

"This is quite an unfortunate affair for both myself and Northrup and probably more so for Northrup. I have been injured at his hands and I have recovered and believe it will be permanent," Dinneen told the court. "This man has got a wife and children and he does not stand alone on that account in this matter. His wife and children will have to suffer with him. They will probably suffer more than he and I will ask the court to be as lenient and merciful to this man as it can for the sake of his wife and children."

"Your plea on behalf of as light a sentence for Northrup is an exhibition of magnanimity that one does not meet with very often," the judge told the chief and questioned Dinneen as to whether he had been influenced by anyone in any way into making the request.

"Everything I do I do of my own free will and voluntarily," responded the chief. "It is sympathy for this man's family, and I took into consideration the condition this man was in when the deed was committed. He was badly under the influence of alcohol at the time."

The chief went on to say that he believed the people of North Adams would feel the lightest sentence possible would be "sufficient punishment" for Northrup.

White again expressed surprise at Dinneen's wish for a light sentence for the man who had shot him three times. Noxon told the judge that, although it was an incident with aggravated circumstances, he didn't want to go against the wishes of the victim in the case.

When Northrup's name was called, he stood up and readied himself to be sentenced. The judge ordered the former policeman to spend at least three years and no more than five years in the state prison in Charlestown. Northrup was handcuffed and taken to the jail in Pittsfield to await transport east to serve his sentence.

Northrup was ecstatic, believing he was going to get a much harsher sentence since the average punishment for this crime during the 1890s and early 1900s ranged from between four and fifteen years (depending on the circumstances), with the average being about an eight-year state prison sentence.

After serving his sentence, Northrup returned to North Adams and settled back into family life with his wife and children. He obviously couldn't return to his prior job and instead became a carpenter. It's worth wondering, and unfortunately wasn't documented, whether Northrup ever ran into his old boss on the streets of the small city.

Northrup died in North Adams on February 12, 1914, of pulmonary edema, a condition caused by excess fluid in the lungs brought on by myocarditis, a heart problem. He was fifty years old.

Dinneen died a little more than a decade later and took the bullet from Northrup's gun with him to the grave.

Part III
ACCIDENTS AND INCIDENTS

The parade in honor of President Theodore Roosevelt's visit makes its way down North Street in Pittsfield on September 3, 1902. *Courtesy of the* Berkshire Eagle.

8
THE TRAIN STATION TRAGEDY

It was the train whistle from a freight train that started the stampede. It was Memorial Day, May 31, 1898, and the crowds were unusually large at the Pittsfield Depot. The Spanish-American War was raging what seemed like a world away, but many of the Berkshires' "boys in blue" were coming home on leave, while others who had been wounded were returning for good. The air was electric that evening as the crowd waited impatiently for the train that carried their loved ones.

Chief John Nicholson, Captain Michael Leonard, two patrolmen and a sheriff's deputy tried to maintain control of the massive crowd, but when a freight train blew its whistle as it approached from the west, everyone believed it was the passenger train and rushed onto the tracks. When the people realized it was the wrong train and it wasn't stopping, it was too late.

The freight train running on the Albany & Boston track was at full speed since no signal had been given to slow it down. When the officers realized the train wasn't slowing, they attempted to push the crowd back onto the platform, but hundreds blocked their path, and they had to force their way through. Leonard rushed forward, plucked a small child from the train's path and pushed a woman back onto the platform as the train rushed toward him.

When the train engineer saw what was happening, he managed to bring the train to a complete stop in very short time, but not before the engine smashed into Leonard's right side, wheeling him around with tremendous force and knocking him unconscious.

A 1906 postcard of the Pittsfield Boston and Albany Railroad Depot. *Courtesy of Wikimedia Commons.*

Edward Lynch, a friend of Captain Leonard, was also injured as he attempted to hold the crowd back as it continued to ripple forward, the people in the rear unaware of what was happening just a few feet in front of them. Lynch had made it onto the platform but was jostled back onto the track just as the train passed. Emma Cogswell was also injured when she was knocked to the track, dislocating her knee. Both Lynch and Cogswell would eventually recover from their injuries.

When the train finally came to a stop, train workers carrying lanterns rushed around the locomotive looking for any more dead or wounded, but thanks to the police officers who had managed to get the crowd out of the train's path, no one else had been hit.

They took Leonard to the nearby police station, and from there, a horse-drawn ambulance transported him to the House of Mercy hospital. Lynch was also brought there. As the terrible news spread throughout the city, Pittsfield's medical men, as well as one visiting from New York, poured into the hospital to see if they could help. But Leonard was in bad shape, his condition beyond the era's medical capabilities. His head had five deep cuts, and his skull was fractured. His face was so swollen on the left side as to be unrecognizable, and his left arm above the elbow and the left hand had been completely stripped of flesh. Four of Leonard's fingers on his left hand had been crushed and had to be amputated. He had numerous broken bones (this was determined by touch since the hospital wouldn't get an X-ray machine for another eight years). It's also likely there was swelling to the brain and a number of internal injuries. The doctors held no hope for his recovery.

While "Cap," as he was affectionately known throughout the city, lay in bed, unconscious and near death, his fellow officers and family crowded into his hospital room and stayed with him until the end. His six children were there, but his beloved Mary, whom he married in 1867, had died a decade earlier of tuberculosis, when she was just forty-five. Three of their other children didn't survive into adulthood.

Born in Ireland on July 22, 1843, Leonard emigrated with his family at age seventeen and settled in Pittsfield. He learned shoemaking, the family trade, from his father, who was a well-known cobbler in the city. Leonard went to work for Robbins & Kellogg, a shoe manufacturer, where he worked with Lynch. But Leonard yearned for a different kind of life, and in 1882, he was appointed as a police officer by Pittsfield's selectmen. He quickly moved up the ladder and was appointed captain of the night shift four years later.

June 1 broke cool and overcast. Leonard died that morning at 9:30 a.m., without ever regaining consciousness. "Kind, faithful 'Cap' to those who knew him best, the news of his sudden death came with the greatest force. It seemed almost beyond credence until the fact that it was a grim reality became known," a local reporter observed.

That day, Mayor William Whiting ordered the city's public buildings to fly their flags at half-staff and called an emergency city council meeting to discuss the matter. Chief Nicholson took care of the funeral arrangements with the help of a local undertaker.

On the morning of Friday, June 3, a steady stream of visitors came to 52 Wellington Avenue in Pittsfield to pay their last respects to Leonard and to try to comfort his children, elderly father and other relatives. Leonard's body was laid out in his home's parlor, where the scent of fresh flowers hung thickly in the air. The casket was of cedar and covered with black broadcloth. A prominent silver plate simply read: "Michael Leonard, Aged 55."

The left side of Leonard's face, which was severely injured, was covered with a white cloth. But the right side of his face was unblemished, and he appeared as if he were merely asleep amid a spray of dark pansies, Leonard's favorite flower, which were placed inside the casket and buried with the officer.

The police department provided two massive flower arrangements. One was in the shape of a broken column with white and pink carnations against a background of green vines with the years of Leonard's service with the department, 1882 to 1898, written in yellow immortelle flowers, while a white dove figurine surmounted the column. The second display was in the shape of a police badge and was made of pink and white roses with the words "Our Captain. Police Department" at the bottom. The Sheriff's Office sent a flower arrangement in the shape of a heart, which stood amid many other bouquets and arrangements from various organizations, agencies and personal friends of Leonard.

At 9:15 a.m., the procession set out from Wellington Avenue and slowly wended its way through the streets of Pittsfield. Leonard's fellow officers were at the front of the line, followed by members of the hose company in which Leonard had served, the family and other officials. The horse-drawn hearse came next. Sheriff Charles Fuller and several others who were riding in a carriage brought up the tail end of the entourage. Residents lined the streets and removed their hats in honor of the fallen officer. The procession ended at St. Joseph's Catholic Church, located on North Street, in the heart of the city.

The mayor and other city officials waited outside the church for the procession to arrive, as did a mass of residents. It was one of the biggest funerals Pittsfield had ever seen. Many of the city's businesses closed for the event, and the mourners in attendance for the "people's friend" were of all classes of citizen, according to the *Berkshire County Eagle* newspaper.

The six police officers who had served on the force longest carried their comrade's casket into the imposing Gothic-style church, the largest in the Berkshires, which had been completed a little more than thirty years earlier and is still there today.

Reverend Father John Fitzgerald stood at the main altar framed by three imposing stained-glass windows as he officiated the solemn requiem high mass. An emotional rendition of the hymn "Nearer My God to Thee" echoed through the large church. Afterward, Leonard's remains were buried in St. Joseph's Cemetery.

Leonard's memory is still honored annually by the Pittsfield Police Department.

TEDDY'S WILD RIDE

On the morning of September 3, 1902, Pittsfield's mayor Daniel England stood on a podium erected in Park Square and introduced President Theodore "Teddy" Roosevelt to a massive crowd of more than ten thousand people. "This day which has brought us a distinguished gentleman will always be remembered with patriotic pride and delight," he enthusiastically remarked.

Unfortunately, the day would instead be remembered for the tragic death of the first Secret Service agent to fall in the line of duty while protecting a president. Roosevelt narrowly avoided being killed as well.

Roosevelt was in the midst of touring New England that fall to rally support for Republican candidates in the region. On the evening of Tuesday, September 2, he arrived in Dalton, Massachusetts, an hour behind

A portrait of President Theodore Roosevelt taken around the time of the carriage accident in Pittsfield. *Courtesy of the Library of Congress.*

Festive bunting and flags decorate North Street for President Theodore Roosevelt's visit. *Courtesy of the* Berkshire Eagle.

schedule from Westfield, Massachusetts; was given a tour of the town; and spent the night at Governor Winthrop Crane's home, where the president was serenaded by local residents. When the sun rose the next morning, it promised to be a beautiful fall day in the Berkshires—warm and sunny with just a hint of a crisp breeze in the air. Roosevelt woke up early and, by 8:00 a.m., was giving his first speech of the day to an excited crowd, including in the front near the podium some overly excited and loud schoolchildren, whom Roosevelt lightly scolded, telling them, "hush now, boys."

By 8:30 a.m., the president's carriage was rolling into Pittsfield to the blowing of whistles, ringing of bells and booming of cannons, which kept up for a full five minutes. Roosevelt was looking splendid in a black Prince Albert coat, light trousers with dark stripes running down the outside of the legs, a dress shirt with a turndown collar, a dark blue four-in-hand tie and a large red rose in his buttonhole.

In Pittsfield, what was originally planned as an unpretentious and simple welcome for the president had, by the day of the event, grown into a full-fledged blowout, with a large parade down North Street featuring Civil War veterans from the various Grand Army of the Republic posts and other patriotic organizations, bands playing martial music and American flags and celebratory bunting hanging from nearly every building, lamppost and tree along the president's route.

The president didn't even bother to sit down as the parade started up near St. Joseph's Catholic Church led by a contingent of city police. He stood in the open landau carriage driven by four horses and doffed his silk top hat while the massive crowds that lined both sides of North Street and filled every available window waved small American flags and handkerchiefs.

The parade ended at Park Square, where the president gave a ten-minute speech on good citizenship and manliness, with an emphasis on the importance of courage, honesty and common sense. Afterward, Roosevelt and a few other dignitaries stopped by the home of former U.S. senator Henry Dawes on Elm Street for a brief visit, and then they got back on the road to visit Southern Berkshire County.

Throughout the day's events, Secret Service agent William "Big Bill" Craig kept a close eye on Roosevelt. Ever since Leon Czolgosz had assassinated President William McKinley in Buffalo, New York, in 1901, which resulted in Roosevelt becoming president, the Secret Service had been tasked with protecting the nation's leader. Craig, forty-six, was the perfect man for the job and was considered one of the best in the service. More than six-feet tall (his height was variously given as between six-two and six-four) and two hundred–plus pounds of muscle, the accomplished boxer, wrestler and swordsman had a distinguished military background that showed in his ramrod-straight posture and martial bearing. Born in 1855, in Glasgow, Scotland, at nineteen, he joined the Royal House Guards, known as "the

The crowds cheer for President Theodore Roosevelt as his carriage rolls down North Street in Pittsfield. *Courtesy of the* Berkshire Eagle.

Blues," the military cavalry regiment tasked with protecting Queen Victoria. He would later see combat in both Egypt and Sudan before immigrating to the United States, initially going to Chicago, where his family had settled. In 1898, he moved to Holyoke, Massachusetts, where two of his brothers were living, and worked for a time as a jailer at the Hampden County Jail.

He joined the Secret Service in 1900 and was eventually assigned to the White House. His large physique and military history belied a gentle soft-spoken quality and sweet sense of humor. Craig enjoyed spending time with the president's family, especially Roosevelt's four-year-old son, Kermit. Craig, whose birthday was only a month away, was soon to marry the actress Katherine Murphy of Washington, D.C., the sister of a well-known actor of the time, Tim Murphy.

As the presidential party headed down South Street toward its next stop, Lenox, Craig sat up front in the landau next to David Pratt, the driver, who was from Dalton. Roosevelt was in the seat facing forward with Governor Crane, while across from them sat the president's private secretary, George Cortelyou, and Congressman George Lawrence. The carriage was surrounded by a mounted guard.

At 9:40 a.m., Roosevelt was chatting with the governor about the beauty of the Berkshires and enjoying the passing scenery as they headed up the foot of what was known as Howard's Hill on South Street, about a mile and a half from Park Square where the president had given his brief address.

The mounted guard behind the presidential carriage saw it first. A trolley from the Pittsfield Electric Street Railway was approaching at a fast clip from the north and appeared as if it was racing to beat Roosevelt's carriage at a nearby crossing that cut directly across the landau's path. The guards attempted to get the motorman's attention to tell him to slow down but were unsuccessful. When Cortelyou saw what was happening, he shouted, "Oh my God!" Crane stood up and began waving his arms to get the motorman's attention. The carriage driver apparently had no idea the trolley was approaching and had gotten the two lead horses across the track when the accident occurred.

"Suddenly we heard the clang, clang, clang, of the trolley gong and before we knew anything else the car had struck us," Roosevelt later recalled.

One of the horses was struck, the front of the carriage splintered, all four wheels were crushed and the entire carriage was thrown several feet. Pratt was pitched sideways off the carriage, while Craig landed directly in the path of the trolley, the wheels passing over his body, killing him instantly. Roosevelt and the rest of the party were thrown from the landau. The president, Cortelyou, Crane and the congressman seemed to have suffered only minor injuries. Pratt was pulled from underneath one of the fallen horses and was seriously injured. The horse had to be put down by a police officer at the scene.

District Attorney John Noxon, who had been one of the passengers on the trolley, hopped off the back of the car and headed over to where Craig

lay. The agent's handsome face was now unrecognizable, his upper body crushed to a pulp, his head split open. In the confusion, people believed the body lying across the tracks was that of the president.

Roosevelt's party walked to a nearby home, where Craig's body was also taken. As the president walked to the house, a cheer went up from the gathered crowd, but he waved it away, telling them, "Don't cheer, one of our party lies dead."

Roosevelt was bleeding slightly from a facial wound but refused any medical attention, telling everyone it was "merely a scratch" and ordering that they focus their attention on the other men. Pratt was taken to the House of Mercy hospital, where it was discovered he had suffered a dislocated shoulder, various sprains and a badly scraped up face. Craig's body was taken by horse-drawn ambulance to a local undertaker.

The president commented that the motorman's actions were an "outrage" and criminal because the trolley was going at such

Top: President Theodore Roosevelt's personal secretary, George Cortelyou. He was slightly injured in the carriage accident. *Courtesy of the Library of Congress.*

Left: Massachusetts governor Winthrop M. Crane, who was with Roosevelt during the crash. *Courtesy of the* Berkshire Eagle.

an excessive speed. "Unless he had lost control of it, I can't see how the motorman could have allowed it to travel so fast at such a time. It came down upon us like a flash," he said after the crash.

Just minutes after the accident, as Euclid Madden, the motorman, stood next to his trolley car, he told a reporter from the *Berkshire Evening Eagle* that the horses had turned directly onto the track and he was unable to avoid the collision. He tried his best to stop, but he didn't have time, he said.

While reporters from the nation's largest newspapers had been following Roosevelt during his New England trip, none were present for the accident, as they had already gone ahead to Lenox. An *Eagle* reporter was first on scene, arriving just after the crash.

The trolley car had been packed with people, mostly the city's well-to-do residents, including James Hull, a director of the trolley company, who were bound for the nearby country club. At least one witness said the riders had urged the motorman to hurry so they could reach their destination before the president, believing he would be stopping there for a moment. It turned out to be nothing more than a rumor, as Roosevelt's schedule did not include a visit to the club.

The presidential carriage was heavily damaged in the crash. *Courtesy of the* Berkshire Eagle.

Onlookers survey the aftermath of the collision involving the presidential carriage. *Courtesy of the* Berkshire Eagle.

Madden and James Kelly, the conductor, were quickly arrested and taken to the Pittsfield police station, although they were not initially charged with any crime.

After about thirty minutes, Roosevelt insisted the tour of the Berkshires continue over the rest of the party's strenuous objections. They had, after all, just been in a serious accident. Cortelyou had an ugly contusion across the bridge of his nose and a wound to the back of the head that dripped blood down the back of his neck and stained his collar red. Roosevelt insisted, and another carriage took them to Lenox, where the president, his face clearly banged up by the wreck, briefly described the accident and Craig's death. "I loved him because of his faithfulness and his kindness to my children," said an anguished Roosevelt, his voice choked with emotion. In Stockbridge, the retinue stopped in front of the Red Lion Inn where a large crowd had assembled. The president again gave the news of the accident. He begged off giving a speech but did take a large bouquet of flowers presented to him. Afterward, the group boarded a train for a short ride to Great Barrington, where a crowd of five thousand people awaited Roosevelt's arrival. The president again made a brief announcement about the wreck. "I beg you to be quiet and I thank you warmly for your reception," he said in a somewhat agitated tone before leaving for Connecticut, the last state on his tour.

Meanwhile, manslaughter charges were filed against the thirty-two-year-old Madden and twenty-five-year-old Kelly. Both men were released on bail, $5,000 ($13,500 today) for Madden and $2,500 ($6,700) for Kelly, pending a hearing the next morning in the district court. The men, described as "faithful and reliable" employees of the trolley company, had been in police custody for eight hours, much of that time without being charged. Madden's brother, a former city alderman, along with a representative of the trolley company, put up the bail money. On Thursday morning, the defendants appeared with Attorney William Turtle, but the arraignment was postponed for two weeks since one of the state's principal witnesses, Pratt, the carriage driver, was still in the hospital. Pratt, as he lay in bed recovering, obsessively spoke about the accident and repeatedly told his doctors he couldn't have avoided the collision.

Madden told reporters he was running his trolley at his normal pace and denied that anyone had pushed him to drive the trolley at an excessive speed. He was adamant that the landau's driver was to blame for crossing the tracks at an unusual spot and at an odd angle that was too close to the trolley. When Madden saw the carriage cross the tracks, he reversed the engine and slammed on the brakes, but it was too late, he said. Several witnesses came forward who were on the trolley and didn't believe Madden was driving recklessly, but if Teddy Roosevelt says you were driving too fast, you were driving too fast. An inquest into the death of Craig was held, and it was determined the trolley had been traveling at an excessive speed and that Madden and Kelly's actions "contributed" to Craig's death. Madden and Kelly were indicted and ended up pleading guilty to manslaughter in January 1903 on the eve of trial. In a deal worked out between the prosecution and their lawyer, Turtle, the men were ordered to pay a large fine, but only Madden served jail time. He was sentenced to a six-month sentence at the Berkshire County Jail and House of Correction.

A day after Craig's death, his two brothers from Holyoke came to collect the body. The governor met them at the train station. Members of the city police, decked out in their dress uniforms, solemnly bore the casket and placed it on the train that would take it to Chicago, where Craig was buried.

Back at the White House, Roosevelt, while talking to reporters, denied he had been badly hurt, likening his injuries to what a man might get from a polo match or "any other sport in which he might unskillfully engage." In truth, he had suffered an injury to his left leg that became painfully infected, required emergency surgery three weeks later and continued to bother him for some time. The president said he would have regarded the crash as "a mere incident of the trip if it had not resulted in the death of Craig. I was genuinely fond of him. He was faithful and ready and I regret his death more than I can say. I regret exceedingly that the New England trip, carried through so delightfully to the last day, should have had such a tragic ending."

Part IV

THE ONES WHO GOT AWAY

10
THE FAILED GREAT BARRINGTON BANK ROBBERY

It was just after 1:00 a.m. on Saturday, May 29, 1875, when Emma Deland woke up to find herself face down on her bedroom floor, her head forcefully held by a strong hand. She was able to turn her head enough to make out three masked men in her room. When she began to scream, one of the men put his face close to hers.

"Keep still, and we won't hurt you, but if you make a noise, we shall kill you," the stranger told her.

The scream had woken her brother, Frederick, who happened to be just the person the intruders were looking for. Frederick was the cashier of the National Mahaiwe Bank of Great Barrington, and they were there to force him to open the vault at the nearby bank so they could take out a very large withdrawal, the kind that's only made by dangerous men.

Frederick jumped out of bed, shouting, "What's the matter, Em?" before he realized what was happening. He was grabbed by the throat by one of the robbers and thrown backward onto his bed. He was handcuffed and questioned.

"I suppose you know what we are after," said one of the men. Frederick, a Medal of Honor recipient for his valor during the Battle of Port Hudson in Louisiana during the Civil War, didn't bother answering. He wasn't scared of these men, but he was frightened by what they could do to his family.

"How many people are there in the house?" one of the men asked. "My father, mother, my sister and our servant, Ellen," he told them, knowing it wouldn't be advisable to lie to these men. (Their elder sister, Mary, had married five years earlier and lived in Pittsfield.)

Downtown Great Barrington today. *Photograph by author.*

Three of the robbers found their way to the servant's room but had a hard time taking Ellen in hand as she "fought like a young tiger," according to one account. They had to carry her down the stairs kicking, biting and scratching the whole way. She was finally gagged and tied up.

Emma, now handcuffed, was ordered downstairs as well and was shoved onto her mother's bed, where the elder woman was already lying and had been likewise cuffed. Their mother, Roxana, begged the men not to mistreat her husband, William, who had suffered a stroke a few months before and was partially paralyzed. They didn't listen, treating the sixty-eight-year-old roughly when tying him up.

Finally, Frederick answered their question. "I know what you want, but you'll be disappointed," he told them. "The bank put in a new chronometer lock on the safe just a few days ago. It's impossible for me, or anyone else, to open it until the hour for which it was set," he told two of the robbers. One went to find their leader. They came back into Frederick's bedroom.

"That story won't go down. We've seen you lock and unlock it just a few days ago, and you'll do it again for us," said the man who seemed to be in charge of the brigands. They took Frederick's keys and ordered him to give them the combination to the outer vault. One of the robbers stayed behind to guard the family, and the other men rode off to the bank.

While they were gone, Frederick's parents were ordered to get up. Emma begged the man to let them stay where they were, as her mother had a broken hip. The robber put his dark lantern (a lantern with a shutter that could be opened to allow a small amount of light to be seen) next to Roxana's face to make sure she was actually an elderly woman. Her feet were fastened to the bed, which caused her some pain. Her husband's legs were also tied to his bed. Emma was ordered onto a nearby chair and was bound to it by the legs. Her arms were still handcuffed behind her, forcing her into an awkward and uncomfortable position. The family was gagged, with Emma's pulled so tight it drew blood.

Twenty minutes later, the rest of the robbers returned. "You've been lying to us about this chronometer lock, you rascal," the leader of the gang said to Frederick when they arrived. "We'll chronometer you."

They forced him to get dressed, tied a noose around his neck and led him out of the house. Once outside, they blindfolded him and took him to the bank. When they arrived, they removed the blindfold, switched his handcuffs from back to front and pushed him toward the bank door. One of the robbers went inside the building with Frederick while the rest remained outside to stand guard.

"I know you can unlock the combination on the vault," the man told him. "Do it right the first time, or things are going to go hard for you."

Frederick unlocked the outer vault, and they walked inside. "We can't go any farther," said the cashier. The crook, still not believing Frederick, put his ear to the inner vault and heard the distinctive ticking of a clock.

Angry now, the man roughly grabbed Frederick. "Come on," he said, pushing him toward the exit. They again blindfolded their prisoner and headed back to the Deland home. The robbers questioned Frederick about the lock that had stymied their plan and about when exactly it had been put in, since they had been casing the bank and had seen him locking and unlocking the vault on Monday. They learned they had been just three days too late.

The lock that saved the day was brand new and came from the Sargent & Greenleaf Company (S&G), based in Rochester, New York. Inventor James Sargent had perfected the chronometer lock in 1873 and received a patent for the device. It was based, at least in part, on a design by Dr. John Berge, who had shown his plans to S&G hoping they'd buy it. They didn't. Instead, like the crooks they were trying to keep out of banks, they stole it—or, at least, heavily borrowed from it. The first of the locks, priced at the equivalent of about $8,200 today, was installed at a bank in Illinois and soon became the standard across the country. The company would later use this foiled crime and a similar one in Barre, Vermont, two months later (likely attempted by the same gang) to advertise their product.

That early morning in May 1875, the leader of the gang told Frederick that these locks were "good for a new thing" but would eventually be able to be cracked.

Back at the Deland residence, the bandits tied up and gagged Frederick, stole bonds valued at more than $50,000 today from William's desk and made their escape. The family could hear the clatter of fast horses going down the road and across the Green River Bridge. It was about 2:15 a.m.

The family was able to work their gags off and began shouting for help, but none came. Finally, Emma was able to maneuver herself close enough to the door. She yanked the curtains aside with her teeth, turned the door latch with her shoulder and pushed the door open. By this time, it was about 4:00 a.m. The family continued calling for help until a neighbor was roused from sleep and stumbled over to see what all the yelling was about.

While the family was attempting to get help, the robbers were making their way unnoticed into Columbia County, New York, which bordered the Berkshires to the west. By the time the authorities in Massachusetts had gotten organized, the crooks were long gone. But over in Hudson, New York, where the gang had rented horses a few days before the attempted robbery, a posse that included the Columbia County sheriff and two city cops, among others, was combing the streets of Hudson near the waterfront. They soon learned that the bandits had just been ferried across the Hudson River to Catskill, a village in Greene County. The party pressed a local fisherman into service and was taken to the east side of the river, where lawmen from Catskill joined in the pursuit. It was soon discovered that the gang had just rented a carriage. The posse eventually caught up with the crooks near the town of Cairo, and a wild shootout ensued. One of the carriages containing some cops was hit, as was a horse, but they fared better than the robbers. One of them was shot in the arm, but the entire gang still managed to escape into the woods and was never apprehended.

The botched bank robbery and ensuing flight was quite a sensation and even caught the interest of Samuel Clemens, better known as Mark Twain, who was then living with his family in Hartford, Connecticut, about eighty miles southeast of Great Barrington. The story of the affair made it into one of the many scrapbooks the writer kept. This was the second attempted break-in at this particular bank. Back in November 1870, several crooks tried to blow the vault open but used too much gunpowder, causing such an explosion that the entire town was roused from sleep. The perpetrators scattered with nary a banknote for their trouble. At least they managed to escape.

The gang that was most likely responsible for the 1875 robbery attempt was made up of some of the best-known brigands of the Gilded Age, including "Big" Jim Brady—also known as "Albany" Jim—Jimmy Hope and Big Frank McCoy, who were responsible for many of era's greatest bank robberies.

Brady was a master of disguise, bold and ruthless, but a careful planner as well. He was connected to the Ocean Bank job in Manhattan in 1869; the Northampton National Bank robbery of 1876, in which about $1.6 million (about $35 million today) was taken; and a string of others in various parts of the country and Canada. Brady's compatriot Hope was involved in the famed Manhattan Savings Institution robbery in 1878 that netted about $78 million in today's terms.

At the time of the Great Barrington attempt, Brady and Hope were on the lam following two daring prison breaks. The first was from Auburn State Prison, in New York, in January 1873. After the escape, Brady, Hope, McCoy and two others were involved in an attempted bank robbery that November in Wilmington, Delaware. Using the same modus operandi as the Great Barrington attempt, the gang held the cashier's family hostage, but the family servant managed to escape and alert the police. The robbers were publicly lashed and given ten-year sentences but managed to escape from a jail in New Castle, Delaware.

By 1900, Brady had been in and out of prison, was washed up and living in what we today call a homeless shelter (but at the time was called an almshouse) in Westchester County, New York, just north of New York City. He claimed to have made millions during his long criminal career and had a mansion in New Rochelle, not far from the miserable living conditions he had come to call home by age seventy-four.

Brady, who may have been the man who had bragged to Frederick Deland that he would one day be able to crack a time lock, complained to a reporter who tracked him down at the almshouse that, although there wasn't a lock he couldn't "pick, wedge or blow," when security systems that used electricity came into use, things really went downhill.

"Electricity—it's in the walls, the floors, wires stuck in where you never think of them," he grumbled. Three years after the interview,

Brady threw himself in front of a passing train and was killed instantly. Frederick Deland, on the other hand, would go on to become president of the Mahaiwe Bank and would pass away in 1922 at the age of seventy-eight.

THE MONEYLENDER DOUBLE MURDER

Hiram Tinney knocked on the door, but no one answered. He looked in the window, knocked again and then stood for a moment wondering where Henry and Blanche could be. Henry Reed's pawnshop and money-lending operation that he ran out of the first floor of his house was pretty much always open for business. It was 8:00 a.m. on a Saturday, an hour and day when the Reeds would usually be more than willing to open their door to a customer, especially to one like Tinney, who needed a $15 loan (around $420 today) and was willing to pay Henry's steep interest rates.

Tinney crossed Webster Avenue and went to the home of David Fairfield, a friend of his. Fairfield told Tinney he hadn't seen the Reeds since Friday evening. Both men returned to the house, went around to the back door, which they found ajar, and went inside. There was a heavy silence within. The men called out to Henry and his older sister, Blanche, with whom he shared the small house, but no one answered.

Inside Henry's room, his clothing was piled on a rocking chair near the bed. The outlines of a large body could be made out under the covers, and a leg covered in thick black hair jutted out rigidly over the side of the bed. They peeled back the sheets and found Henry laying face up, a pillow soaked with blood obscuring his features. A bloodstained carpenter's mallet lay on piano stool near the bed.

Leaving Tinney behind, Fairfield left the house and ran to the police station. When the police arrived on that day, August 7, 1897, they made a search of the rest of the residence. Upstairs, they found Blanche face

WHERE BLANCHE REED'S BODY WAS FOUND.

The spot where Blanche Reed's body was discovered. *Courtesy of the* Berkshire Eagle.

down on the floor, her body splayed out in the open doorway of her bedroom. She had been shot four times, the bullets entering her head and neck. A very short time later, the crime scene was alive with people. Two deputies, four North Adams patrolmen and the chief of police, as well as several reporters and local doctors, were tramping through the house looking for clues. By the time the medical examiner, Orland J. Brown, arrived at about noon, there were also several hundred curious residents outside the house in a state of excitement that only tragedy seems to stir up. Brown kicked out everyone, except two doctors and four officers, and began making his observations of the Reeds' bodies and of the state of the house.

Henry, fifty-five, had a number of blunt force wounds to the head, his face had an expression of utter horror and there was a gag in his mouth. Brown determined the murderer had beaten Henry to death with the mallet. They next examined Blanche's room. There was a large pool of blood under her partially clothed body and, strangely, an accordion. The sixty-eight-year-old had apparently landed on it when she was shot. The police surmised Blanche had woken up, began to get dressed as she walked toward the open doorway and was shot by an unknown assailant who was on the staircase leading to the second floor.

The accordion made a little more sense as they examined the rest of the small house, which was stuffed with musical instruments, including pianos, organs, guitars and drums. Henry had once been a dealer in musical instruments but had turned to the more lucrative trade of pawnbroking. In regard to this later pursuit, the space not taken up by instruments was filled with everything from cheap pocket watches to rubber boots to bonnets to old furniture.

The house had been completely ransacked. The bureau drawers were pulled out and dumped onto the ground, trunks were left open and the clothes from the closets pulled out, but then, it was somewhat hard to tell the difference between what the burglars had done and the typical state of the place. Today, the Reeds would likely be called hoarders. By the time the medical examiner had finished at the house, three state police detectives, as well as a representative of the district attorney's office, had arrived to aid in the investigation.

The bodies were removed later that day, and autopsies were conducted. Brown determined the murder took place between 1:00 a.m. and 3:00 a.m. based on the rigidity of the bodies and the state of the partially digested food observed in the Reeds' stomachs during the autopsy. Now, it was a matter of figuring out who did it and why. Initially, police believed the killing was motivated by revenge but soon learned Henry Reed had been holding a large amount of cash on him connected to the purchase of a farm. They had the why, but the more the investigators looked into the dealings of Henry Reed, the more they realized there were literally hundreds of suspects. It seems everyone wanted Henry Reed dead.

Henry was considered a "sharp man" by the city's residents, who believed his main goal in life was acquiring money, and scruples were not part of the equation. At the time of his death, it was reported he was worth about $500,000 in today's terms. Originally from Vermont, Henry and his sister had come to North Adams more than twenty years before. He soon acquired the nickname "Black Reed" because of his swarthy complexion and his temperament. He was a powerfully built six-foot-tall man with a profusion of dark hair on his chest and arms. He wasn't known as a flashy dresser but wore nice clothes and often mingled with members of the city's business community. He kept his professional dealings close to his ample vest and steered clear of conversing about his business. He kept careful accounts, and any one of the hundreds of people listed in the records was a potential suspect. The police began the nearly impossible job of sorting through the list of possible perpetrators as well as following up on the tips, rumors and wild speculations that began to pour in from residents.

Reed had made a lot of enemies over the years, and there was seemingly no end to the vitriol from locals concerning his business practices. He kept his property in his sister's name so he could skirt any debts he had himself accrued, but he charged excessive rates on loans he made on farms, equipment, livestock and even household goods and "was always ready to exact his pound of flesh," according to a *Berkshire Evening Eagle* reporter. Henry had no pity for those desperate enough to accept his terms, and if a customer missed a payment, he'd seize the property. Henry "would rather grind a dollar out of a debtor than earn two by labor," a local resident was quoted as saying.

There were even dark whisperings that the Reeds' home became a blind tiger, or speakeasy, at night where the area's boozers could trade stolen items, whatever wasn't nailed down really—from kid gloves to books to bolts of silk and satin—for a drink at steep prices. It was said that an item that may have been worth a dollar would only buy a drink that cost a dime at Henry's place.

A coroner's inquest into the killings saw 125 witnesses but no real answers. Among the many potential killers the police looked at, Horace Lanfair, a fifty-eight-year-old carpenter from Clarksburg, was initially the prime suspect. He was a close friend of Henry Reed with whom he did a lot of business. The pair had been seen together the afternoon before the murder. Reed had loaned his friend some money, using Lanfair's horse and buggy as collateral, and Reed was busy trying to sell the items in order to get the money Lanfair owed him. Lanfair was questioned by police on several occasions but never arrested.

There was also a man in Stamford, Vermont, who had threatened to kill Reed after having his house foreclosed on a year earlier, but he, too, had a solid alibi.

A report that a young man was seen jumping a fence into the Reeds' yard on the night of the killing didn't lead anywhere. The man showed up at the police station and told officers he was taking a shortcut to his father's house a street over from the Reeds. His story checked out, and another possible lead was squelched.

Other suspects included Charles Bonai, a former resident of Great Barrington, who at the time was on the run with David Week. The men were wanted in connection with the July murder of George Nichols near Bridgeport, Connecticut, that was committed in the midst of a break-in. The pair had been seen in the vicinity of North Adams around the time of the Reed murders. Bonai was later hanged for the Nichols murder, but before he died, he told police that Weeks had been responsible for a second, earlier murder in Huntington (now called Shelton), Connecticut. Weeks was sentenced to life in prison after pleading guilty to second-degree murder in regard to the Nichols killing. It's unclear whether either man was ever questioned about the Reed murders.

The last person to see the Reeds alive, besides the killer or killers, was Lillie Crosier, who stopped by to visit Henry and Blanche around 7:30 p.m. that Friday. She was a family friend of the Reeds and, as a gifted musician, was often asked by Henry to test out the various musical instruments he still sold from time to time before he would deliver them to customers. That night, in an eerily portentous conversation, Blanche and Lillie discussed a frightening murder making the headlines across the country that summer. Blanche dwelled on the circumstances of the murder of William Guldensuppe, a Turkish bath attendant, whose torso and arms, neatly wrapped in oilcloth, had been discovered by some children playing on the shore of the East River in New York City. The killers in that case, the victim's girlfriend and her lover, had been arrested that July, and the papers were full of the lurid details of the crime. Little did Blanche know that she, too, would soon be fodder for the press. That night, Lillie also mentioned to Henry that the back window next to the door should be locked since "anyone could slide that screen and reach in his hand and withdraw the door bolts and come in."

"Oh, there's no danger of that," Henry replied.

"Well, I'd be scared to sleep in this house with the window screen that way," retorted Lillie.

"I'd just as soon lie down here and sleep with my revolver underneath my head and all the doors wide open as sleep with them closed. You know I always keep my revolver under my pillow," said Henry.

During her visit with the Reeds, Lillie thought she heard footsteps nearby. They stopped talking and listened, but the sound had stopped. A few minutes later, they again heard the noise, and they determined it seemed to be coming from the next yard over. Nothing more was said of it, and Lillie left soon afterward.

It's possible Henry's revolver, which was never found, was used to murder Blanche, according to police, since the only gun in the house recovered by investigators was located in Henry's room, tucked away in a drawer, covered in dust. It hadn't recently been fired.

Lillie also recalled Henry mentioning that some men would be coming by to settle a business matter with him later that night, and he wanted Blanche to handle it. Blanche told Lillie that Henry seemed to be afraid of these men and always had her deal with them.

The most relevant information the police were able to collect came from Fairfield's wife, who heard "a number of noises" she hadn't "taken particular notice to at the time" that seemed to come from the back of the Reed place that Friday night and early Saturday morning. It began with the barking of a neighbor's little black-and-tan dog followed by a noise like "someone stamping upon a soft surface." She then heard something that sounded like "a horse striking his hoofs sharply against the sides of his stall." Ten minutes later, as she stared out the window, eating a donut and drinking a glass of milk, she saw a buggy roll by with a single occupant. She couldn't make out his features, but he wore a light colored hat and a dark suit.

A few minutes later, she saw another man hurrying up the street in the direction the buggy had taken. Police surmised the noise the woman heard, far from being the common sounds of a horse in its stall, were in fact those made during the murder. They believed the loud striking noise was the report of a small-caliber pistol. If true, this would place the murder occurring between 12:45 a.m. and 1:00 a.m. Two other witnesses who happened to be up around that time were walking down the street after having a nightcap on the front porch of a nearby boardinghouse when they saw a buggy race by and commented that the driver seemed to be in quite a hurry. The men didn't see anyone on foot. The buggy was traced to Stamford, Vermont, where the trail went cold.

The case stalled, even with the $1,800 ($50,000 today) reward being offered for information, and it wasn't until 1900 that more information about the mysterious horse and buggy surfaced. The coroner's inquest was dusted off and resumed. Two men from Scotland by way of Clarksburg, Massachusetts, on the Vermont border, soon became the prime suspects.

David King and Alexander Grant were witnesses during the 1900 inquest, and on June 23, King was arrested during the inquest's final session by state police investigator George Dunham. Grant was allowed to leave and then taken into custody on the street.

There was an odd reticence on the part of Attorney General Hosea M. Knowlton to deal with the Reed affair after the investigation pointed to Grant and King as the perpetrators. Knowlton, who had been the lead prosecutor in the infamous Lizzie Borden case in which she was acquitted of the axe murders of her father and stepmother in 1892, refused to pull the trigger on arresting King and Grant. District Attorney Charles Gardner brought the evidence the investigators had collected to Knowlton who "did not feel like assuming the responsibility of pushing the case," according to Gardner. But since the attorney general was now backed into a proverbial corner, he ordered Detective Dunham to look into the matter further; however, it was Gardner who ended up ordering the suspects' arrests without Knowlton's consent.

The evidence against King and Grant revolved around the latter's purchase of a farm in Clarksburg from Henry Reed for $1,300 (about $36,000 today) with a mortgage of $1,250 ($35,000) that Grant was supposed to repay in small amounts. The sale wasn't recorded anywhere, which was strange, considering the careful books Henry kept. The two friends both worked in North Adams, Grant as a baker and King at the Arnold Print Works, one of the largest producers of printed fabrics in the world (the contemporary art museum MASS MoCA is now located on the site). They rode to the city together on a daily basis, and Grant would often park his buggy at the Reeds' house. The prosecution contended that they had witnesses who placed the two suspects in North Adams on the night of the murder, but both men claimed to have been home in Clarksburg when the crime was committed. Police believed Grant and King were aware that Reed had a large amount of cash on hand and that the motive for the murders was simple greed.

Grant, forty-one, had moved from his native land to Rhode Island eleven years earlier, where he met King, thirty-six, who was also originally from Scotland. The two men became boon companions and, at the time of their arrests, were living together on Grant's farm in Clarksburg, along with Grant's wife. Now, the two men were sitting in jail in North Adams facing the possibility of death in the state's electric chair. The prisoners were moved to the county jail in Pittsfield in preparation for grand jury proceedings in mid-July. Grant's accommodations were in cell seventy-three, the infamous "murderer's cell" where William Coy and John Ten Eyck had both spent their last days on Earth before being hanged. King's cell was on a separate floor above the guardroom. The men could at least take comfort in the fact they were more than ably represented by the former district attorney Charles Hibbard and attorney Clarence Niles of North Adams.

Gardner presented the case to the grand jury in July and trotted out about sixty witnesses in the largest proceeding of its type at the time. While the case was circumstantial, it was fairly solid, or so the prosecutor believed, and Gardner expected that an indictment for first-degree murder would be issued. To everyone's surprise—even that of the defendants—the grand jury failed to indict the pair.

"There were some sixty witnesses called for the hearing before the grand jury. I think the evidence has been very carefully developed, and every effort made to apprehend the perpetrators of the crime. The evidence bearing on the men's guilt was of such a nature that the case seemed a proper one for a grand jury," Gardner told reporters after the news broke.

The DA called the case "one of the most singular" and "unusual" he had ever come across since there seemed to be so many clues that led to a variety of suspects that it was "hard to determine who was the guilty party."

Mrs. Grant was overwhelmed by the news and reiterated her oft-voiced opinion that her husband was innocent. She had remained devoted to Alexander throughout the ordeal.

After the grand jury proceedings, a reporter from the *Berkshire Evening Eagle* approached the two men. "Have either Mr. Grant or Mr. King anything to say regarding the good news?" he enquired. Both men responded that they were innocent and that this fact had sustained them through the ordeal. They were gratified by the outcome but never doubted it would end in acquittal. They went on to say they didn't hold a grudge against the police or prosecutors who were doggedly pursuing the case in an attempt to solve "the mystery surrounding the tragic deaths of the Reeds."

As for these gentlemen," Grant, his voice heavy with emotion, said in his lilting accent, indicating the two defense attorneys, "we cannot say too much. They have been kind, very kind, and have done all in their power for us."

As they headed back to the North Adams jail for a final night of incarceration before being formally released in district court the next day, North Adams police chief William Dineen (who would be shot by one of his patrolmen three years later) didn't even bother handcuffing them.

Dineen told reporters that he believed the two men would be indicted but would ultimately be found not guilty of the crimes, an opinion that either showed the chief didn't think much of the evidence, the prosecutor's abilities or both. Niles told reporters that since very little evidence is needed for a grand jury to "hold a man for trial, the evidence of the Commonwealth in this matter must have been very slight indeed."

Detective Dunham said that it hadn't been the strongest case but was solid enough to take to trial. "It is a good one considering that it is based purely on circumstantial evidence," he told newsmen.

There was a crowd of curious residents at the Pittsfield station, where Grant, King and the chief boarded a train heading north. Everyone wanted a last look at these infamous men whose names had been so prominent in the local papers for weeks and had even received national attention due to the horrific nature of the Reed murders.

Downtown North Adams, Massachusetts. *Photograph by author.*

The next day, the men were formally released. A large crowd of their supporters met them outside the North Adams police station, and they were received with a great cheer. Grant and King were free after spending close to a month in jail with the possibility of death sentences hanging over their heads. They returned to Clarksburg that day.

Many people believed more clues would be found and another arrest made, but it never happened. If Grant and King were not behind the murders, then the killings were never solved. Over time, the story of the murders faded from memory, along with the Reeds' home and even Webster Avenue, destroyed more than fifty years ago during a period of urban renewal. What remains are the graves of Henry and Blanche Reed in Manchester, Vermont, and the fact they never received the justice they deserved.

Part V
AXES AND BARKERS

A country road through the Berkshire Mountains. *Courtesy of the Library of Congress.*

12

THE OTIS AXE MURDER

ART

Charles Wood sat in jail in Pittsfield finishing up an elaborate piece of what would later come to be called folk sculpture but, in 1877, was referred to as a piece of "whittling." It was large, eighteen inches by twenty-four inches, and included a swing of elaborate openwork, a technique that involves cutting away pieces of wood for a decorative effect. A four-inch-tall galloping horse, described as "a really spirited piece of carving" by a local reporter who got to see the sculpture, was in the center of the swing. On one side of the piece there was a carved anchor with fancy latticework and a gracefully curved roof with a slender flagstaff. On the other side sat a two-inch-tall column with a winding staircase of twenty-three steps featuring bannisters and a rail that led to a Swiss arbor that surmounted the whole piece. The reporter couldn't stop talking about it.

"It shows a wonderful patience and an unusual skill in the use of tools," he gushed.

Wood had used a knife, a nail, a needle and some sandpaper to create his masterpiece, which he presented to the sheriff on the eve of Wood's murder trial. If the prisoner had been as focused and creative about trying to escape the confines of the jail as he had been in creating the intricate piece of carving, he might have had a good chance of slipping away. After all, he had access to a variety of sharp objects that he could have used to try to bust his way out of the joint. But Sheriff Graham Root trusted Wood, who had

Otis, Massachusetts, today. *Photograph by author.*

been a model prisoner since he arrived five months earlier. Wood showed no visible signs of apprehension about his upcoming trial. He remained as cheerful and quiet as ever and was "quite elated by the pleasure the sheriff manifested in receiving" the sculpture, according to the reporter.

While Wood's handiwork displayed a keen sense of refined skill, he hadn't been so light-handed the previous September when he picked up an axe and brutally murdered a little old lady in Otis who had invited him in to warm himself by the fire during a torrential rainstorm.

MURDER

On the afternoon of September 10, 1876, Jeptha Hazard sat in his home with his wife as a storm raged outside. Suddenly, a strange man burst through the door without knocking.

"I'm cold and I want to warm myself by your fire," he told him. "I'm almost froze through."

Jeptha gave him the man a chair, which he placed near the fire. The man, who had a French accent, began chatting with Jeptha and his wife, Hannah.

His name was Charles Wood; he was a Frenchman by birth and was an itinerant farmhand who was tramping through the area. He seemed nice enough, asking how the old couple's health was before finally enquiring how far Kendall Baird's tavern was from their place. Wood then stood up to leave and headed for the door, but as he reached the doorway, he instead walked past it and began fumbling through a stack of tools that included a hoe, a pitchfork and an axe. Wood picked up the hoe and swung it at the older man, striking him with the handle side in the chest and shoulder. Jeptha ran out the door and began calling for help from the neighbors. Wood then struck Hannah with the hoe, knocking her from her chair before retrieving the axe and hacking the woman to death.

A neighbor, George Tillotson, rushed into the house with the old man after hearing Jeptha's calls for help and was nearly hit by an axe blow from Wood, who was still inside the house. Tillotson was able to disarm Wood, but the two continued to struggle until, with a mighty effort, Tillotson threw Wood to the ground and held him there until more neighbors arrived. Tillotson was slightly wounded in the scuffle.

Hannah Hazard's tombstone in the Otis Center Cemetery in Otis, Massachusetts. *Photograph by author.*

Jeptha found his wife lying on the floor in a pool of blood with deep gashes in her head. One of Wood's axe blows had landed behind Hannah's left ear and entered her skull, killing her.

"Not a quarrelsome word had passed between us," Jeptha would later testify in court. He seemed dumbfounded that this happened after he had allowed Wood to warm himself in his home and had showed him nothing but kindness.

Wood initially lied about his name, telling the assembled crowd he was John Mayon but, eventually, gave his true name. George Tillotson's wife tried to force Wood to look upon Hannah's body, but he steadfastly refused. He told his captors he didn't know why he had just murdered the old woman and repeatedly said he wished he was dead.

TRIAL

The day that Wood was presenting his "whittling" to the sheriff, his lawyers, Timothy Spaulding, a Northampton attorney just out of law school, and Herbert Joyner, a much more seasoned defense attorney from Great Barrington, arrived in Pittsfield around noon and went to the jail to meet with the defendant. It's not clear from the various news stories whether this was their first meeting—one would hope not, for the sake of their client. The two men then retired to the law library, where they prepared their strategy. Spaulding would later be involved in a less-than-honest land transfer in which the sister of the famous poet Emily Dickinson was the victim.

Meanwhile, Massachusetts attorney general Charles R. Train (who had served as volunteer aide-de-camp to General George B. McClellan during the Civil War) and District Attorney Edward H. Lathrop also arrived in the city and met at the American House Hotel, where the DA briefed the attorney general on the details of the case. This was a time when the state's attorney general actually handled certain high-profile cases.

Dr. George C.S. Choate arrived the same day from New York. He was an expert who planned to opine on whether the defendant was insane or not. He ran a private mental asylum in Westchester County, New York, whose claim to fame was having housed the well-known New York newspaper editor and owner Horace Greeley (who famously uttered

"Go West young man") at the time of the newspaperman's death. Before running Choate's Home for Insane and Nervous Invalids, he was in charge of Massachusetts's largest asylum, located in Worcester. The good doctor spent some time examining the prisoner to "test his mental capacity and soundness," according to one of the local papers. It was all for naught, as Choate wasn't called to testify at the trial.

Wood slept well that night. At 8:30 a.m. on February 6, 1877, he was transported to the Berkshire Superior Court in Pittsfield for trial. It was quite a spectacle at the new courthouse. Every seat was filled for the proceedings, which looked to be chock-full of shocking details surrounding the gruesome killing, with hopes that more details would emerge concerning the mysterious Frenchman accused of the murder. The ladies in attendance were given the most comfortable seats from which to view the proceedings and get a closer look at the defendant, who was described as "a rough looking fellow of 25 years of age" by the newspapers.

Reverend William MacGlathery, from Pittsfield's St. Stephen's Episcopal Church, said a prayer to the assembled throng before jury selection began. During the selection process, Wood ran the show for the defense and would loudly declare to the court in his French-accented English, "I don't want him," concerning any of the potential jurors he didn't like and would smile as the man was removed. While the prosecution only refused two potential jurors, Wood used almost his entire allotment of challenges—twenty-two—before a jury of twelve men was finally seated.

"No doubt these were all much obliged for their escape from the unpleasant duty," a reporter quipped about the men who were excused from jury duty. This was a time when juries were sequestered during deliberations no matter how long it took to decide a defendant's fate, and in this case, that fate included the very real possibility of hanging. Judge James D. Colt allowed the chosen jurors to pen quick letters to their families and work, letting them know they would be unavailable for some time.

DA Lathrop gave his opening statement and then immediately called the victim's husband to the stand. Mr. Hazard told the jury how his and his wife's kindness had been repaid with bloodshed. Other prosecution witnesses included neighbors and the coroner, who went into detail about Mrs. Hazard's wounds. He told the jury that three of the wounds penetrated the skull, while several others "bit into the scalp."

In an unusual move, the prosecution called Judge Moses Pease, who had overseen Wood's initial arraignment on the murder charge in the police court in Lee shortly after the killing. The judge testified that, at the hearing, Wood initially pleaded guilty to the murder charge and had been very matter of fact about killing the old woman. Because the lower court wasn't allowed to handle murder cases, a not-guilty plea was entered for Wood that day so that the case could make its way to the higher court.

The defense team, trying its best with what appeared to be an open-and-shut case for the prosecution, described the killing as an act of self-defense on the part of their client. They trotted out several witnesses who testified to Wood's previously quiet and harmless character. Wood also took the stand.

Wood told the jury he was born and raised in France and had been in the United States for about a decade and in Massachusetts for four years.

That morning, Woods was in Russell, Massachusetts, to try to collect some money he was owed. He then set off for West Stockbridge. Along the way, he picked up a large stick, about the length of a cane, for protection against roaming dogs. The weather had been rainy and blustery that day and, by the afternoon, had become a torrential storm, so he stopped at a random house, knocked and was greeted at the door by an old man.

"Can I get out of the rain?" Wood recalled asking Jeptha. Once inside and sitting by the fire, the old man talked about his health, which was poor, and told Wood he'd been out hunting that day and was tired.

"The old man was deaf and told me to speak up," Wood told the jury.

The defendant testified that Mrs. Hazard passed him a bottle of medicine and told him to taste it. When he did, he immediately felt sick and got up to leave.

"Seeing a stick by the door, I took it and struck the old man twice for I was mad they had given me the medicine that made me sick," he told the jury.

When Mr. Hazard ran out the door, Wood said he went to retrieve his hat, which had fallen onto the stove. It was then, he said, that the old lady grabbed the axe to strike him with it.

"I told her to let me go for I was sick, but she stood in front of the door and would not let me leave," he testified. "I seized the axe from her."

The two tussled before Woods grabbed a hammer and began hitting her with it. She fell to the ground, and that was all Woods said he could remember.

"The medicine made me sick and crazy," he said, telling the jury whatever the old couple had given him affected him for "three or four weeks after" the incident.

During cross-examination, he denied ever having killed before "that he knew of," but admitted he had previously been arrested for drunkenness.

Mr. Hazard again took the stand to refute Wood's version of events. He said no one had given the defendant any medicine and that Woods had not even interacted with Mrs. Hazard before the killing.

In his closing argument, Joyner didn't deny his client had killed Mrs. Hazard but argued the circumstances didn't fit the charge of first-degree murder but were more in line with the charge of manslaughter. The lawyer said the old couple had given his client a patent medicine they were in the habit of taking that made Wood sick and that, as the defendant left the home, he decided to give the old man a whack not to seriously injure him but to "learn him not to give nauseating doses [of medicine] to the next weary wayfarer who should ask an hour's hospitality."

Joyner's defense wasn't a bad one. This was a time when medicines were not regulated, and many were mostly alcohol and contained everything from opiates to cocaine, so the possibility his client had been adversely affected by what he said he ingested made for a pretty good circumstance the jury could hang its hat on to keep Wood from swinging at the end of a rope. Joyner told the jury his client only wanted to leave but that Mrs. Hazard attacked him with the axe and that Wood killed her with the hammer in "frantic self-defense." There was no evidence of "motive or malice," and without these things, the crime could not be first-degree murder, the defense attorney opined.

Attorney General Train told the jury that the "malice and premeditation" only needed to have been formed an instant before Wood committed the crime. He said Mr. Hazard's version of events was the true story: that Wood first knocked the old woman from her chair with the hoe before attacking Mr. Hazard and then got the axe with which he murdered Mrs. Hazard. He asked the jury to make sure that the law "throws it protection over the humblest homes and the humblest persons," referring to the Hazards.

Judge Colt then explained the differences between the various degrees of murder and other bits of law before sending the men off to deliberate.

The members of the jury, after their free lunch, began to look over the evidence and debate the merits of the case with the result that eight men were for second-degree murder and four for first-degree murder. The four jurors were looking for a verdict that "would put a rope around the prisoner's neck," one reporter observed. After a few hours of wrangling, the jury found Wood guilty of second-degree murder. Train asked the court to immediately sentence the defendant. Judge Colt ordered Wood confined in state prison for life with one day to be served in solitary confinement.

Wood was stoic as the judge handed down the sentence and had had a similar demeanor throughout the three-day trial. Wood had a lot of time—twenty years, in fact—to think about how a split-second decision changed his life forever. He died at the Charlestown State Prison when he was forty-six on May 18, 1897.

13

THE ROGUE ROMEO

THE SHOOTING IN THE SHADOW OF THE CHURCH

In the shadow of the Seventh Day Adventist Church in Savoy, Massachusetts, Herbert Blanchard argued with Francis Starks, the father of Blanchard's sweetheart, Clara, who wanted the twenty-three-year-old to stay the hell away from his fourteen-year-old daughter. On that sweltering Sunday morning in July 1877, Starks had accosted Blanchard, mad about an article in the local paper that made him and his daughter look bad and which he believed his daughter's paramour had something to do with. Starks felt the information, which was false, came from Blanchard or that he had pushed the reporter, with whom Blanchard was acquainted, to write the piece.

The two went back and forth until Blanchard had had enough. "If you don't stand back I will hurt you," Blanchard said to the elder man before swinging his fist into him and knocking him to the ground. While only five feet, ten inches tall and of a spare build, Blanchard was strong. As the two men scuffled, their fellow parishioners gathered around to watch. When Blanchard pulled a revolver, Francis's brother Albert jumped in and grabbed Blanchard, wrapping one arm around the man's neck and wrenching the arm that held the weapon.

Francis Barden and George Bourne, friends of Blanchard, dragged Albert off their companion and held him as Blanchard let off a shot. The bullet entered Albert's side, traveling through his lung.

Albert, his adrenaline pumping, got shakily to his feet and then groaned in pain. "Blanchard, you shot me!" he exclaimed.

"He served you right," retorted Bourne. "You had no business to touch him."

As Albert stood in a daze, Blanchard shot his brother in the stomach. Francis also managed to get to his feet and began running. Blanchard took aim and let go with two more shots, neither hitting its target.

He then turned back to Albert and ordered him to his knees. Albert obeyed, his hands in the air. Before anything more could happen, Blanchard's father stepped in and, with the help of several other men, got the pistol away from his son.

But Blanchard was far from being stymied in his mad pursuit for blood. He ran into Bardon's house and emerged with a double-barreled shotgun and "started out to slaughter more of the little congregation," according to one news report. Some there said he threatened to shoot two others, including a female parishioner, before his father once again forcefully removed the weapon from his son's grasp.

Strangely, no one tried to stop Blanchard from leaving. He ran from the area and caught up with Francis's son, who was heading to get a doctor for his father and uncle. Blanchard threatened him, and the teenager, too scared to resist, allowed Blanchard to ride with him on his wagon out of town.

Savoy, Massachusetts. *Photograph by author.*

But Blanchard, instead of hightailing out of the county, spent several hours chatting up nearby residents he knew, bragging about what he had done. No one seemed to believe the story. He ate dinner two and a half miles from the scene of the crime before heading to Vermont to stay with relatives.

It wasn't until that evening that any of the congregation bothered to tell the authorities about the shooting affray. When the sheriff finally got wind of it, a large contingent of law enforcement officers from both Massachusetts and Vermont, with some local townsfolk thrown in—every man heavily armed—began to hunt down Blanchard, who was said to be familiar with every mountain ravine and road for miles around. Through torrential rain, the men searched into the night and, by the next morning, had tracked him down to Readsboro, Vermont, at the home of his aunt, about twenty miles from Savoy.

The men surrounded the house while the sheriff of Charlamont, Massachusetts, stepped up and knocked on the door. Just as the door swung open, Blanchard was seen peeking through a window at the rear of the house and was soon in custody and headed back to face justice.

Bardon and Bourne were released after the court found there wasn't sufficient evidence to show they were culpable of the crime.

Adventures Past and a Bleak Future

Blanchard sat in jail awaiting trial, unable to make the $6,000 bail (nearly $13,000 in today's terms) set in the case. He had read every book in there, and since he was well versed in the Bible, he didn't bother rereading that text. It was the nights that were the worst.

He lay awake thinking about the many adventures he had before the Savoy affair curtailed his freedom.

Born in Williamstown, Massachusetts, he was a restless youth, and at fourteen, he ran off to Troy, New York, and enlisted in the U.S. Army under the false name of "Ambrose Keith." He was sent out West as part of Company C of the Third Artillery. He told a reporter he was stationed at Fort Phil Kearny, near present-day Buffalo, Wyoming, during Red Cloud's War and was there at the time of the so-called Fetterman Massacre. Blanchard said he had been out on patrol on December 21, 1866, just a few miles from where Captain William J. Fetterman and eighty soldiers fought—and lost to—a combined force of Sioux, Cheyennes and Arapahos numbering at

The so-called Fetterman Massacre of December 21, 1866, during Red Cloud's War. Herbert Blanchard claimed he had been stationed nearby and was out on patrol at the time of the battle. *Courtesy of the Library of Congress.*

least one thousand and perhaps double that number. Fetterman, a Civil War veteran with no experience in fighting Native Americans, was duped into chasing a small decoy band into an ambush. Among the Native warriors that day was an Oglala Lakota named Crazy Horse who would later participate in another famous battle at Little Bighorn.

Blanchard said he and some other soldiers returned to the fort just after the battle. This near miss may have convinced him the army life wasn't for him, because he deserted after just seven months of soldiering. His lack of soldierly duty was in sharp contrast to that of his father and four uncles, who fought for the Union in the Civil War, with two uncles dying for the cause.

Blanchard eventually made his way back to Hawley, Massachusetts, where his father lived, but soon left for more adventurous parts. He shipped out on the *Kate Allen*, running guns to the Cuban rebels during the Ten Years War, the first of several attempts by the Cubans to throw off the chains of Spanish colonial rule.

He again returned to Hawley and married a girl named Jane, but it was a short-lived affair, mainly because of her father, a "religious fanatic" who took sport in hunting Blanchard with a shotgun. Added to this was the boredom of married life with a girl whose personality was a little lackluster for Blanchard's tastes.

"She was a wooden sort of girl," Blanchard later recalled. He left her to work on the building of the Hoosac Tunnel in the area of North Adams, a dangerous project that had killed nearly two hundred workers over it's twenty-five-year construction. The central shaft of the tunnel would eventually run for nearly five miles under the Hoosac Mountains, the rock blasted and drilled out, as part of the route of the Troy & Greenfield Railroad.

Next, Blanchard headed to California and then into Mexico, where he joined up with the Federalist army and fought under General Juan B. Catina, the "Red Robber of the Rio Grande," who was then supporting President Benito Juárez against Porfirio Díaz, who had declared war on the government after losing the presidential election to Juárez, his old comrade. After being wounded in the head in battle, Blanchard moved on once more, marrying again (it was unclear if he'd even bothered to divorce his first wife), this time to the daughter of a rancher in Durango, Mexico. After his wife, Matlenia, died giving birth to their daughter, Blanchard left the child with the woman's relatives and headed back to California.

He denied the stories being put out by the press that he had killed a U.S. marshal while in California, escaped from prison or ran a faro bank, a mostly crooked gambling racket. He said he worked several jobs, from mining to the mails, before once again taking to sea. Two years later, he was back in the Savoy area, locked up and desperately yearning for his freedom.

"I'm a great lover of nature," he told a reporter, "and it comes very hard to be shut up here in 'murderer's row' as some of the prisoners call it without a glimpse of any green thing and only the sky to look at."

Blanchard believed his troubles stemmed mostly from the jealousy the locals—"Hayseeds," he called them—felt for him. He considered Bourne and Bardon typical of the area's inhabitants—"good honest kind of fellows" who lacked "git' up and git'" and wanted to keep him, "a stylish sort of a chap who is a little fast," away from the local girls.

A *Berkshire County Eagle* reporter admitted that Blanchard—with his light complexion, brown hair and cool gray eyes—had good looks and style and was "not at all an evil looking chap."

"It appears to be true that girls, and some of the womanly age, seem to have been fascinated with him, either for his bravo style, his adventures, which he relates most attractively, or for his personal appearance, which is bright and smart," wrote the journalist.

But there was also a dark side to Blanchard. Clara Starks would later recall an incident leading up to that bloody Sunday. During one of the lovers' clandestine meetings, Blanchard boasted that if he saw her father coming over the hill at that moment, he would shoot him down.

In Blanchard's defense, the Starks were no innocents and may have been responsible for an ambush of Blanchard as he left one of his meetings with Clara just days before the Savoy shooting. As he walked home, Clara's brother at his side, a shot rang out and a bullet whizzed by Blanchard's head. A dark figure rose from a clump of bushes and shot again, the bullet again wide of its mark. Blanchard gave chase but was unable to catch the man. He believed it was one of the elder Stark's relatives who had pulled the trigger and that Francis was behind it since the man had told many in the town that Blanchard would never have his daughter.

A CLOSE CALL AND PRISON TIME

The following January, Blanchard was indicted on felonious assault, his two victims having pulled through thanks to their strong constitutions. Blanchard's lawyer said as much and thanked God for it. Blanchard narrowly missed being charged with murder, especially in the case of Albert Starks, who lay near death for weeks after the shooting. A few days after the affray, he told his version of events at the behest of the authorities, who wanted it on paper in case he died.

On his day in court, Blanchard wore a nicely cut black dress jacket with a purple tie. His wavy hair was parted in the middle, and his mustache was neatly trimmed. His mother, Mary, came from Springfield to be with her son. One newsman described her as a "tall, prosperous looking woman of notable appearance" and guessed she was about forty years old. She was dressed all in black for the occasion. She and Blanchard's father had split up years ago, and she had done well for herself in the intervening years.

There was some back and forth on whether Blanchard would go to trial. With so many witnesses to the shooting, a trial wasn't likely to go well for the young man. In the end, he decided against a trial. When asked by the clerk how he pleaded to the charges, he said "guilty" in a strong, unwavering voice.

The next day at sentencing, Blanchard's lawyer, Abiathar Preston, argued that the fact that his client carried a gun was nothing unusual—it was a "privilege of civilization"—and everyone in Savoy walked around armed to the teeth. The lawyer pointed out to the judge that at an earlier hearing in Adams, the victims' family showed up to court bristling with weapons.

Preston told the court his client and his friends, and those of Clara's family, had fisticuffs in a meadow—before the shooting—and had worked out their differences, with Blanchard staying away from the girl afterward. On the Sunday in question, he said, Blanchard had pulled a gun "while they were squirming and wrestling in a heap." His client's behavior afterward, he admitted, was frenzied and included shooting into the crowd that had gathered. The lawyer called the gunfire "miscellaneous and harmless."

Somewhat unusually, the prosecutor chimed in on Blanchard's behalf, telling the court that the events of that day were chaotic and that witness testimony was conflicting, some saying Blanchard was the aggressor and others that it was Francis Starks who attacked first. There was some evidence that Albert Starks was choking Blanchard and that was why he had pulled his gun.

The prosecutor said that, at the time of the shooting, public opinion was much against Blanchard but that, since then, it had changed; now there was a great deal of sympathy being expressed for the defendant. One wonders if it was being expressed by the women of the county whom, at least according to newspaper accounts, had turned out in their Sunday best to get a look at Blanchard in court that day. The spectators, many of whom were the friends and family of the Stark brothers, were disappointed they wouldn't get to see a trial. Before sentencing, Blanchard gave a long and impassioned speech in which he claimed he had only shot the men in self-defense, but the judge was not swayed, telling Blanchard he had gone too far and sentencing him to six years in state prison. Blanchard would later die at age thirty-five of heart disease while in prison in 1891 for an unrelated case.

14

THE TROLLEY CAR KILLINGS

The motorman, George Hoyt, gruffly told the man to step back and sit down until the trolley car had come to a complete stop. Fadlo Mallak, a Syrian-born millworker, had just requested to get off the trolley and had stepped up to the front door too soon for Hoyt's liking. It wasn't an uncommon request on the Berkshire Street Railway Company line, but that day, something in Mallak that had been bubbling inside, curdling and slowly rising suddenly exploded into violence.

J.J. Mooney, a Pittsfield resident enjoying a ride up to North Adams with his wife, saw Mallak board the car. "He looks like a crazy man," he murmured to his wife, who was seated next to her husband.

What happened on the afternoon of July 22, 1911, would become one of the earliest recorded mass shootings in Massachusetts. It would leave three dead, five wounded and the Berkshires, and beyond, in shock.

It was a bright, sunny day—warm but not overly hot—and the trolley car was full, mainly with women and children, totaling about sixty passengers. Mallak, after weeks of being semi-catatonic—barely speaking and walking around aimlessly as if in a trance—pulled a Colt .38 automatic pistol from his coat, and without a word, pointed it at Hoyt as the driver focused on the road ahead. The trolley car was nearly at full speed as it made its way to North Adams from the neighboring town of Adams.

Mallak fired twice, with one bullet striking the forty-eight-year-old Hoyt, ripping through his back and killing him almost instantly. Mallak then turned on his fellow passengers, who began to scream in panic and confusion. Ten

The Eclipse Mill in North Adams where Fadlo Mallak worked at the time of the shooting. Photograph by Lewis Hine. *Courtesy of the Library of Congress.*

shots rang out. Martha Esler, sitting in the second row of seats, immediately crumpled and fell onto the floor, dead. A bullet had struck her in the right arm, traveled up into her shoulder socket and pierced her lung. Her elder sister, Selma, was struck in the thigh by a bullet as she kneeled down by her dying sister's side. Victoria Sovie was also shot in the thigh as she leaned over to check on Martha Esler. Victoria's sister, Margaret, was wounded by bullets that hit her in the face and arm. Selma, Victoria and Margaret all survived the terrible day's events.

Kate Shea, sitting in the fourth row, was hit in the face by one bullet and struck in the arm by another. Her friend Katherine Hanrahan, sitting next to her, was uninjured. When the firing started, Hanrahan hid under the seat and tried to pull Shea down with her but was too late.

When Mallak began firing, Mooney pulled his wife to the ground and covered her with his own body. He looked up over the seat at Mallak, who appeared to be firing randomly. Mooney mustered up the courage to stand and lunge at Mallak, grabbing the arm that held the deadly pistol. Georgie Hall then began pummeling Mallak with her umbrella before Mallak broke Mooney's grasp and leapt from the car. Mooney had succeeded in wresting the pistol from the killer, but not before Hall was struck in the side by a bullet. The fifty-eight-year-old Adams woman died less than a month later in the North Adams Hospital from her wound.

"She was the real hero," Mooney later remarked to reporters.

Alice Bryant, sitting in the third row next to Hall, was hit in the neck but lived.

There were conflicting stories as to who stopped the train as it took a corner at full speed, nearly running off the rails. Two witnesses believed it had been Hoyt, the motorman, who was able to pull the brake before succumbing to his injuries. Others said it was the quick-thinking conductor, twenty-eight-year-old Arthur Cross, who rushed forward and pulled the brake.

Henry Thomas, a weaver from Adams, standing at the rear of the car, first thought the gunshots were merely the electric lines that ran the trolley cracking, as they often did, but seconds later, he realized Mallack was shooting down the car from the front, emptying the revolver before jumping from the train. Thomas joined the other men who had also jumped off to catch the murderer.

The men gave chase, and one threw a rock that struck Mallak in the back of the head. He turned on the group, pulled a stiletto on them and threatened the men. When one of the pursuers overtook him, Mallak dropped the weapon, stopped running and was captured. He was bound with rope by the men who stood guard and waited for police. Officers from the North Adams police department soon arrived, and it was a good thing for Mallak that they did, since a large, angry crowd had begun to gather and there was talk of lynching the prisoner.

Meanwhile, back at the train, those who hadn't been injured helped the dead and dying. W.T. Nary, the superintendent for the trolley company, arrived at the scene (after commandeering a car from a passing motorist) and took charge, ordering Cross to stay with motorman Hoyt's body, which had just been removed from the trolley. Nary ordered another employee to drive the train to North Adams at top speed. The train picked up a local doctor a short distance up the line, who began working on Mrs. Hall. The woman was laid out on one of the seats and in bad shape. A horse-drawn ambulance arrived and left with Selma Esler, who was apoplectic, incessantly screaming that her sister was dead, even as she was whisked away. The trolley once again began hurtling northward, with a newspaperman acting as conductor, and the superintendent on the lookout for any doctors who might have heard about the shootings and were rushing to the scene to help. Many of the dazed passengers sat quietly during the ride while others wept. The wounded moaned in pain.

When the trolley arrived in North Adams, doctors and nurses poured onto it to help care for the wounded passengers. It was Saturday, and the city was thronged with people who began to crowd around the trolley. A nurse from New York City who happened to be visiting North Adams that weekend pushed her way through the crowd and yelled up to a police officer who was trying to maintain order. "I'm a nurse," she shouted at the officer, who grabbed her by the arm and hauled her aboard. When asked for her name later by a newspaperman, she refused to give it, telling him "nurses do not need to have names."

Mallak was taken to the Adams Police Station for booking, and it was there that the story of how this tragedy came to pass was told. Mallak came to the Berkshires from Syria at about age sixteen and had been in the country about four years before the killings. He worked in the spinning room of one of the many mills of North Adams. He attended night school and was reportedly quiet, even-tempered and had no bad habits but for occasionally drinking beer and chain-smoking. It was the latter habit that led to him ending up with the .38, which he had procured by sending in coupons that came in the cigarette packs, redeemable for the weapon.

Six months before the shooting, Mallak's behavior began to disintegrate. At work, Mallak would suddenly stop what he was doing and burst out laughing. When asked what was so funny, he would refuse to answer and merely return to the job at hand. He began to talk to himself and would accost the female workers, which was noted as being extremely unlike him.

At home, he refused to help pay for the household's needs, a 180-degree turn from his usually helpful behavior. He mostly stopped sleeping, but when he did, he slept fitfully and would wake crying or laughing and unable to explain why. He began wandering from home at odd hours, staying out for long stretches as he walked without aim. He began missing work as well.

Just two months before the tragedy, Mallak's elder brother, Joseph, took him to see a doctor who prescribed medicine to combat his nervousness and sleeping problems. At the time, the doctor suspected that there were mental health issues at play but nothing was done.

Because of his brother's odd behavior, Joseph looked into buying him a ticket on a passenger ship back to Syria and had actually secured passage for Mallak on a ship set to sail that Monday, but it was too late. Mallak, delusional and under the belief people were trying to hurt him, violently lashed out. Unfortunately, his phantoms had coalesced into reality.

The twenty-one-year-old sat at the Berkshire House of Corrections in Pittsfield in the infamous murderer's cell, reserved for prisoners accused of vicious crimes. That August, Mallak once again fell into a state of complete indifference to his surroundings. Two psychiatrists, at the behest of Berkshire Superior Court judge John C. Crosby, went to the jail and examined the prisoner. Drs. George Tuttle, of the McLean Insane Hospital in Waverly, and John Houston, superintendent for the Hospital of the Insane in Northampton, interviewed the prisoner with the help of his brother, Joseph, who acted as an interpreter. Joseph was also there to provide further background to the medical men. During the interview, Fadlo showed an "absolute indifference" to the men's questions and denied the killings or even owning a gun. He said he didn't understand the penalty for murder and couldn't understand why he was being detained. Later in the interview, he became angry and accused his brother of keeping him locked up because Mallak caused trouble at home. The doctors conducted other interviews, including one with North Adams police chief Willian Dinneen, who described Mallak as "indifferent," showing no agitation or excitement just minutes after the shooting.

The doctors diagnosed Mallak with dementia praecox, a somewhat newly recognized disease that had been given this name in 1891 by Arnold Pick, a psychiatry professor at Charles University in Prague, which was then part of the Austro-Hungarian Empire. The term was popularized by German psychiatrist Emil Kraepelin, who also studied this mental disorder. The disorder would eventually be reinterpreted and renamed schizophrenia.

On September 9, 1911, a hearing was held before Judge Crosby in which the doctors described in detail their findings concerning Mallak's mental state. During the proceedings, Mallak seemed unaware of his surroundings and was apathetic as to what was going on around him. Before he was brought into court, he was allowed to speak to some of his family, including his long-suffering brother Joseph, who had stood by Fadlo throughout the ordeal and had always been somewhat of a father figure to his younger siblings. It was unclear what had happened to their father, but by 1911, he was not living with the family. Their grandfather, an influential Syrian army major, died in that country before the family emigrated. Joseph owned a confectionary shop on Union Street in North Adams and helped support the family.

The Syrian community in North Adams, apparently afraid that they would be singled out for abuse, loudly proclaimed the Mallaks were not Syrian but rather Turkish Muslims who were "accustomed to all the injustice, disorder and cruelties practiced in that country which is constantly filled with tumult."

The doctors opined that Mallak's mental disorder would become "more and more profound" and "discernible" as time went on. Crosby asked Dr. Houston about Mallak's rampant cigarette habit (the press often made

Fadlo Mallak, the Syrian-born millworker who shot up a trolley car in 1911. *Courtesy of the Berkshire Eagle.*

mention of this) and wondered if it was possibly a contributing factor to his downward spiral.

"He had been smoking cigarettes excessively but people don't go insane from smoking cigarettes do they?" the judge asked.

Dr. Houston's response was somewhat strange. "Some small boys do," he told the court.

After listening to the experts testify, District Attorney Christopher T. Callahan told the court that, while they were unwilling to concede Mallak was insane, they had "no evidence to offer on the matter at this time."

Judge Crosby made his determination, finding that there was "only one conclusion that can be arrived at and that is that Mallak is insane and ought to be committed to Bridgewater for further observation and examination, there to await further orders of the court."

Mallak was sent to the state's mental hospital for the criminally insane in Bridgewater, about thirty miles south of Boston. Bridgewater was a sprawling complex that began life in 1855 as a state almshouse for the poor of all ages who were wards of the state, either through economic circumstance or "immoral behavior." By the 1890s, it was under the control of the state Board of Lunacy and Charity and had begun housing the criminally insane. By then known as the State Farm, it was both a working farm and prison. Although the state had begun sending the criminally insane there prior to 1895, in that year, the legislature formalized the process, mandating that "all male prisoners who are announced insane after an examination are removed, if the Governor so decides, to the State Asylum for Insane Criminals which is a department of the State Farm at Bridgewater."

In Massachusetts, before 1899, criminally insane prisoners were released after serving their prison sentence, whether they were still considered dangerously mentally ill or not, but following a state Supreme Judicial Court decision, that changed, and mentally ill prisoners could be held even after serving a sentence. If deemed to be still dangerous, they would be held under civil commitment laws until they were determined to be able to be released back into society.

In 1911, when Mallak was sent there, the State Farm housed more than 8,000 patients, with a daily average of about 2,600, including those deemed criminally insane and others sent to the facility for such crimes as vagrancy, drunkenness, "tramping" and "offenses against morality" through three separate departments: alms, prison and insane. The conditions there were bad, with abuse and neglect rampant at a time when there were few treatment options.

Mallak remained institutionalized through the entrance of the nation into the First World War in 1917—he filled out a draft card and gave his reason for non-service as "insane"—and was still there in 1920. During his time there, many changes occurred at the facility. In 1919, it had been placed under the jurisdiction of the Bureau of Prisons and saw a drop in numbers, believed to be due to the war, with resulting losses in agricultural production at the facility. There had been changes in Mallak's personal life as well. His mother had died while he was hospitalized, and another of his brothers, Said, had returned to Syria.

A decade after being declared insane, the doctors there found him competent to stand trial, and in January 1921, he was back in Berkshire County and facing a jury for the killings. He had been indicted for murder in January 1912, but no action had been taken until doctors found him sane enough to stand trial. Over the course of his time at Bridgewater, he was examined several times and continued to show improvement, so much so that he was returned to the Berkshire County Jail. His brother Joseph had, by this time, settled in Connecticut and was still in the candy business. He came up to Pittsfield for the trial and spoke with Fadlo, who told him he had no memory of the shooting and most of the three months prior to the event. Joseph's devotion to his brother was unwavering, seeing to his brother's comforts as best he could at Bridgewater and securing a lawyer for the trial.

The history of the judicial system and the modern insanity defense can be traced back to the early nineteenth century in England after a sensational assassination attempt by Daniel M'Naghten on Prime Minister Robert Peel. Peel was unhurt, but his secretary was killed. At trial, M'Naghten, who believed Peel wanted him dead, was found not guilty by reason of insanity, with the resulting furor ending in a change of the insanity defense laws. In what would become known as the M'Naghten Rule, the insanity defense only applied if the accused was "labouring under such a defect of reason, from a disease of the mind, as not to know the nature and quality of the act he was doing; or, if he did know it, that he did not know he was doing what was wrong." This idea would migrate to the United States and remains the standard today.

Billed by the *Berkshire Daily Eagle* as possibly the shortest murder trial in Massachusetts history, the presentation of evidence took seventeen minutes, with the jury returning its verdict of not guilty by reason of insanity after twenty minutes of deliberations. The prosecution presented two witnesses. The first was Henry Thomas, who had been on the trolley car that day and helped capture Mallak. Dr. Frank Carlisle, the director of Bridgewater, was the second witness. He described how the defendant was insane at the time of the killings and was sane now.

The twenty-nine-year-old Mallak was stoic and said nothing to the jury. He knew he would be heading back to Bridgewater, his home for the last decade. But ten months later, on December 15, 1922, with no fanfare—the newspapers didn't even cover it—Mallak was released from the institution, according to state records. His trail runs cold after this, and it seems plausible that his family sent him back to Syria as they had intended to do before the tragic events of July 22, 1911.

BIBLIOGRAPHY

B esides the sources listed here, I relied on a variety of birth, marriage, military, death and travel records found through Ancestry.com as well as in the Berkshire Athenaeum in Pittsfield, Massachusetts.

INTRODUCTION

Boltwood, Edward. *The History of Pittsfield, Massachusetts: From the Year 1876 to the Year 1916*. Pittsfield, MA: 1916.

Cook, Waldo L. "Murders in Massachusetts." *Publications of the American Statistical Association* 3, no. 23 (1893): 357–78.

"History of the Jury System in Massachusetts." Court System. http://www.mass.gov/courts/jury-info/mass-jury-system/history.

CHAPTER 1: THE GENTLEMAN BURGLAR

New York Evening Herald. "Masked Burglars Held for Trial." January 2, 1894.

New York Evening World. "Says She Was Not Poisoned." July 20, 1894.

———. "Warrants for Two." January 1, 1894.

New York Sun. "The Gentleman Burglar's Trial." July 25, 1894.

New York Times. "Bridgeport's Burglars Well Known." March 4, 1894.

———. "Burglars Awaken Two Girls." November, 18, 1893.

———. "Cord Meyer Dead, Victim of Poisoning." October 15, 1910.

———. "Cord Meyer's Sisters Robbed." December 23, 1893.

———. "Gentleman Burglar Found Guilty." July 25, 1894.

————. "Mrs. Field's Costly Watch Recovered." May 3, 1894.

————. "Stockbridge Is Under Arms." September 10, 1893.

Vermont Phoenix. "Massachusetts Notes." August 3, 1894.

Weeks, Lyman Horace, ed. *Prominent Families of New York; Being an Account in Biographical Form of Individuals and Families Distinguished as Representatives of the Social, Professional and Civic Life of New York City.* New York: Historical Company, 1893.

CHAPTER 2: THE CUCKOLD KILLER

Berkshire (MA) Evening Eagle. "George Huber Sentenced." January 11, 1904.

————. "New York Man Shoots and Kills Young Wife." September 15, 1902.

Boston Evening Transcript. "Battis and Huber Pardoned." December 22, 1910.

Brooklyn (NY) Daily Eagle. "Pardons Too Easy." December 25, 1910.

Commonwealth of Massachusetts. *Attorney General's Report for 1904.* Boston, MA: Wright & Potter Printing Company, 1905.

Milwaukee (WI) Journal. "Crazed by Grief." October 13, 1902.

New York Evening News. "Wife Murderer Is Pardoned." December 22, 1910.

New York Evening World. "Killing of Wife Huber's Second Murder." September 15, 1902.

New York Times. "Aged Pair Striken by Huber's Pardon." December 24, 1910.

Pittsfield (MA) Sun. "Arraigned in Court this Morning." January 11, 1904.

CHAPTER 3: THE MURDER THAT NEVER WAS

Berkshire (MA) Evening Eagle. "Eloped or Murdered." July 17, 1879.

New Bloomfield (PA) Times. "A Relieved Man." November 30, 1880.

New York Times. "Shufelt Missing Wife." July 14, 1879.

Pittsfield (MA) Daily Evening Journal. "The Shufelt Mystery." November 18, 1880.

Pittsfield (MA) Sun. "Great Barrington." July 16, 1879.

CHAPTER 4: THE RAILROAD MEN AXE MURDER

Berkshire County (MA) Eagle. "All Is Over." March 3, 1893.

————. "Another Setback." February 25, 1893.

————. "Confession at Last." October 12, 1891.

————. "The Coy Exceptions." February 24, 1893.

————. "Coy Is Indicted." January 21, 1892.

————. "Coy's Chance Gone." February 20, 1893.

————. "The Last Chance Gone." March 1, 1893.

———. "Murder Most Foul." October 15, 1891.

———. "Now the Defense." March 24, 1892.

———. "The Whalen Murder." October 29, 1891.

Commonwealth of Massachusetts. *Attorney General's Report for 1893*. Boston, MA: Wright & Potter Printing Company, 1894.

Fessenden, Franklin G. "Improvement in Criminal Pleading." *Harvard Law Review* (1896): 105–7.

Paddock, Frank K. "The Coy Murder." *Transactions of the Massachusetts Medico-Legal Society* 2 (1898): 123–7.

Plumb, Charles Sumner. *A Biographical Directory of American Agricultural Scientists*. Knoxville, TN, 1889.

Reno, Conrad. *Memoirs of the Judiciary and Bar of New England for the Nineteenth Century*. Boston, MA: Century Memorial Publishing, 1901.

Shattuck, Dr. George A., ed. *The Boston Medical and Surgical Journal*. Vol. 128. Boston, MA: Cupples, Upham & Company, 1893.

Chapter 5: The Thanksgiving Day Double Murder

"Before the Final Bar." *Albany Law Journal* 56 (1898): 232.

Berkshire County Sheriff's Office. "Berkshire County Sheriff's Office History." http://www.bcsoma.org/page_mobile.php?PageID=525&PageName=Berkshire+County+Sheriffs+Office.

Childe, Hamilton. *Gazetteer of Berkshire County, Mass., 1725–1885*. Syracuse, NY: Journal Office, 1885.

Commonwealth of Massachusetts. *Acts and Resolves: Passed by the General Court of Massachusetts: January Session*. Boston, MA: Wright and Potter, 1839.

———. *Attorney General's Report for 1878*. Boston, MA: Wright & Potter Printing Company, 1879.

Cook, Waldo L. "Murders in Massachusetts." *Publications of the American Statistical Association* 3, no. 23 (1893): 357–78.

Massachusetts Court System. "James D. Colt." http://www.mass.gov/courts/court-info/sjc/about/reporter-of-decisions/james-d-colt.html.

New York Times. "A Negro Murderer Hanged," August 17, 1878.

Ten Eyck, John. *The Life of John Ten Eyck*. Pittsfield, MA: David O'Connel, 1878.

Vermont Phoenix. "David Stillman and Wife," December 7, 1877.

Washington Evening Star. "Exhibiting a Murderer's Dead Body, at Ten Cents Admission Fee," August 17, 1878.

CHAPTER 6: THE CARD GAME KILLING

Berkshire County (MA) Eagle. "A Serious Shooting Affair." November 2, 1878.
———. "At the Jail." November 9, 1878.
Davis, William Thomas. *Bench and Bar of the Commonwealth of Massachusetts.* Vol. 1. Boston, MA: Boston History Company, 1895.
Hoosac Valley (MA) News. "William A. Montgomery." April 10, 1879.
New York Herald. "Murderers Indicted." January 17, 1879.
North Adams (MA) Transcript. "Adams Murder Case." December 26, 1878.
———. "Ellis Recovery Improbable." December 12, 1878.
———. "George Ellis." November 14, 1878.
———. "Montgomery." January 9, 1879.
———. "Probably a Murder." November 2, 1878.

CHAPTER 7: THE BLOODSTAINED BADGE

Bennington (VT) Evening Banner. "Chief Shot Three Times." December 8, 1903.
Berkshire (MA) Evening Eagle. "Dinneen Will Live." December 18, 1903.
———. "Dinneen Saved Northrup." January 11, 1904.
———. "Officer Northrup Dropped from Force." December 19, 1903.
Marquis, Albert Nelson. *Who's Who in New England.* Vol. 1. Chicago, IL: AN Marquis, 1909.
New York Times. "Patrolman Shoots Chief." December 18, 1903.

CHAPTER 8: THE TRAIN STATION TRAGEDY

Berkshire County (MA) Eagle. "A Brave Officer's Death." June 1, 1896.
———. "Honored His Memory." June 3, 1896.
Boltwood, Edward. *The History of Pittsfield, Massachusetts: From the Year 1876 to the Year 1916.* Pittsfield, MA: City of Pittsfield, 1916.
Commonwealth of Massachusetts. *Municipal Register for the City of Pittsfield for 1899.* Pittsfield, MA: Journal Office, 1899.

CHAPTER 9: TEDDY'S WILD RIDE

Berkshire County (MA) Eagle. "Inquest at Once." September 6, 1902.
———. "Inquest Opened." September 9, 1902.
———. "Motorman and Conductor Before the District Court." September 4, 1902.
———. "President Roosevelt's Visit Marred by Fatal Accident." September 3, 1902.

Bishop, Charles Owen, and Chip Bishop. *The Lion and the Journalist: The Unlikely Friendship of Theodore the Electrical World and Engineer*. Vol. 40. New York: McGraw Publishing Company, 1902.

Garrett, Manning. "Old Money from the National Mahaiwe Bank Of Great Barrington." antiquemoney.com. http://www.antiquemoney. com/national-bank-notes/massachusetts/old-money-from-the-national-mahaiwe-bank-of-great-barrington-1203.

New York Times. "President's Landaue Struck by a Car." September 4, 1902.

Roosevelt and Joseph Bucklin Bishop. Guilford, CT: Globe Pequot, 2011.

Sacred Heart Review. "Six Months in Jail and Fine." January 24, 1903.

Street Railway Journal. Vol. 21. New York: Street Railway Publishing Company, 1903.

CHAPTER 10: THE FAILED GREAT BARRINGTON BANK ROBBERY

Bacon, Edwin Monroe. "Men of Progress: One Thousand Biographical Sketches and Portraits of Leaders in Business and Professional Life in the Commonwealth of Massachusetts." *New England* (1896): 639.

———, ed. "Men of Progress: One Thousand Biographical Sketches and Portraits of Leaders." *Bankers Magazine* 68 (1904): 281.

Berkshire County (MA) Eagle. "Bold Attempt at Bank Robbery." June 3, 1875.

———. "Brief Locals." November 24, 1870.

Bolivar (TN) Bulletin. "The Boss Bank Burglar," November 26, 1886.

Byrnes, Thomas. *Professional Criminals of America*. New York: GW Dillingham, 1895.

Coy, Simeon. *The Great Conspiracy: A Complete History of the Famous Tally-Sheet Cases; Also, Incidents of Prison Life, Notorious Criminals and Their Crimes; Reflections Upon Prison Reform, Etc.; Together with a Brief Recital of the Personal and Political Life of the Author*. Indianapolis, IN: self-published, 1889.

The Financier, January 2, 1875, 267.

Freeland (PA) Tribune. "Famous Crook Dying." November 26, 1900.

Goldsmith, Meehna. "Time Locks: A Piece of Watch History." Longitude: Christie's Blog for Collecting Watches. http://blogs.christies.com/longitude/watches/time-locks-a-piece-of-watch-history.

New York Daily Graphic. "Bank Robbery." July 9, 1875.

Salt Lake City Herald. "The Wages of Sin." June 3, 1903.

Shilling, Donovan A. *Made in Rochester*. Victor, NY: Pancoast Publishing, 2015.

Taylor, Charles James. *History of Great Barrington (Berkshire) Massachusetts*. Barrington, MA: Town of Great Barrington, 1928.

Washington Times. "Death Claims Old Man Hope." June 11, 1905.

CHAPTER 11: THE MONEYLENDER DOUBLE MURDER

Berkshire County (MA) Eagle. "The Inquest Adjourned." August 14, 1897.

———. "Murdered for Revenge." August 10, 1897.

———. "Tracing the Single Team." August 8, 1897.

———. "Two Person Murdered." August 7, 1897.

———. "Was Robbery the Motive?" August 9, 1897.

Berkshire (MA) Evening Eagle. "Grant and King Will Go Free." July 13, 1900.

———. "The Trial of the Murderer." February 8, 1877.

Brown, O.J. "A Case of Double Homicide: Its Mystery." *Transactions of the Massachusetts Medico-Legal Society* 3 (1899): 18–23.

Commonwealth of Massachusetts. *Annual Report of the State Board of Charity of Massachusetts, Volume 15.* Boston, MA: Wright & Potter Printing Company, 1879.

———. *Annual Reports of Various Public Officers and Institutions for the Year 1876.* Boston, MA: Wright & Potter Printing Company, 1877.

———. *Attorney General's Report for 1878.* Boston, MA: Wright & Potter Printing Company, 1879.

Gordon, Lyndall. *Lives Like Loaded Guns: Emily Dickinson and Her Family's Feuds.* New York: Penguin, 2010: 287–90.

New York Times. "Arrest for Murder in North Adams." June 24, 1900.

———. "Bonai Says Weeks Did It." December 15, 1897.

Red Cloud (NE) Chief. "A Murder Mystery." July 27, 1900.

CHAPTER 12: THE OTIS AXE MURDER

Berkshire Evening (MA) Eagle. "Brutal Murder." September 21, 1876.

CHAPTER 13: THE ROGUE ROMEO

Anderson (SC) Intelligencer. "A New England Tragedy." August 23, 1877.

Berkshire County (MA) Eagle. "January Session of the Grand Jury." January 17, 1878.

———. "A Tragedy in Savoy." July 9, 1877.

Brown, Dee Alexander. *The Fetterman Massacre.* Vol. 523. Lincoln: University of Nebraska Press, 1962.

Howes, Marc "The Hoosac Tunnel, Florida—North Adams, Massachusetts." www.hoosactunnel.net.

Richardson, Chad, and Michael J. Pisani. *The Informal and Underground Economy of the South Texas Border.* Austin: University of Texas Press, 2012.

Troy (NY) Daily Times. "The Savoy Tragedy—Deposition of Albert M. Starke." July 15, 1877.

Ziegler, Vanessa Michelle. *The Revolt of "The Ever-faithful Isle": The Ten Years' War in Cuba, 1868—1878*. Ann Arbor, MI: ProQuest, 2007.

CHAPTER 14: THE TROLLEY CAR KILLINGS

Berkshire County (MA) Eagle. "Mallak to Be Tried for Murder of 10 Years Ago." January 19, 1921.

Berkshire (MA) Evening Eagle. "Considered Case of Mallak." January 8, 1912.

Brown, Gino. "Pittsfield Division/Berkshire Street Railway Co." Berkshire Street Railway Company. http://gino.cdfw.net/_trolleypage/Hoosick/page2.html.

Commonwealth of Massachusetts. *The Bridgewater Correctional Complex, 1855–1987: A Policy Report of the Senate Committee on Ways and Means*. Boston: Commonwealth of Massachusetts, November 1987.

———. *Thirteenth Annual Report of the Board of Prison Commissioners of the Massachusetts*. Boston, MA: Wright & Potter Printing Company, 1914.

Dercum, F.X. "Dementia Praecox." *Journal of the American Medical Association* 44 (1905): 355–7.

"Member Murdered by Infuriated Foreigner." *Motorman, Conductor and Motor Coach Operator*, 1910, 29–30.

New York Sun. "Kills Two in Trolley Car." July 23, 1911.

New York Times. "Mallak Shot at Conductor." July 24, 1911.

Pittsfield (MA) Journal. "Hearing on Mallak." September 1, 1911.

———. "Mallak Goes to Bridgewater." September 9, 1911.

———. "Mallak in Murderer's Cell at Berkshire House of Correction." July 24, 1911.

———. "Sanity Experts See Mallak." August 30, 1911.

ABOUT THE AUTHOR

Andrew K.F. Amelinckx is an award-winning crime reporter, freelance journalist and visual artist. He grew up in Louisiana and now lives in New York's Hudson Valley with his wife, Kara Thurmond, and dogs, Boo Boo and Bingo.

He is a contributing editor for the magazine *Modern Farmer* and the former crime and courts reporter for the *Berkshire Eagle* newspaper. He holds an undergraduate degree from the University of Louisiana in Lafayette and an Master of Fine Arts in painting from Pratt Institute in Brooklyn, New York. He sits on the editorial board of the Columbia County Historical Society and is a member of Investigative Reporters & Editors.

Author photo by Robert L. Ragaini.

Printed in the USA
CPSIA information can be obtained
at www.ICGtesting.com
LVHW020740060923
757299LV00006B/108

9 781540 212481